Rhythm

What It Is and How to Improve Your Sense of It

Rhythm

What It Is and How to Improve Your Sense of It

Andrew C. Lewis

EIGHSEIGH PRESS

First published in 2005 by Eighseigh Press
1050 North Point, Suite 1504
San Francisco, California 94109
Rhythmsource.com

Editor: Tad Lathrop
Design and Production: Nancy Carroll
Music Typesetting: Don Giller

Library of Congress Control Number: 2005901633

ISBN 0-9754667-0-4

Manufactured in the United States of America

1 2 3 4 5 6 7 8 9 / 11 10 09 08 07 06 05

Music is composed of two elements, pitch and rhythm;
of the two, rhythm is the more important.

Beulah Forbes (1918–2003)
San Francisco Conservatory of Music

Contents

BOOK 3 ADVANCED RHYTHM STUDIES

BOOK 4 RHYTHM IN PERFORMANCE

Acknowledgments

Thanks to my colleagues, friends, conductors, and teachers, whose teachings and tips over the years are the basis for this book. Special thanks to David Garner, Marilyn Burns, Fred Euphrat for the book's opening line, and Justin DiCiccio for the drumset exercise in Book Three. Also thanks to Tad Lathrop, whose intuitive, creative editing made the process a pleasure.

Foreword

Rhythm is a huge word and a huge subject. It's a concept, a metaphor, a timetable for daily activity, a descriptor for fluidity in sports, the key to cycles in nature and all life.

Rhythm is the backbone of art. In the realm of the sonic art, music, rhythm was succinctly described by Charisius, a Roman grammarian ca. 400 A.D.: "Rhythm is flowing meter, and meter is bonded rhythm."

It's fascinating to muse on the concept of rhythm/flow, and how mutable it is from culture to culture, and indeed, from style to style within a culture. Getting from point A to B to C to D in Western classical music is quite a different journey than in Afro-Cuban or Brazilian music, where language and dance can influence the forward and backward inflections of rhythms (and melody and harmony). As harmony is not a component of Indian classical music, it is rhythm that forms the basis of its architecture. Absorbing the rhythmic components of a culture can reveal so much about its makeup, its art, its food, and its people. (The sharp angles in the Afro-Cuban-based clave of New Orleans funk can offer a hint to the spices in Cajun/Creole cuisine, as the relentless four-note rhythmic motif of Beethoven's Fifth Symphony can shed light on thematic development for all Western art.)

Rhythm clearly exists in many flavors and notions, and in this book Andrew Lewis has taken up the enormous task of breaking down its components into deliverable parts to foster the development of a keen *sense* of rhythm in tandem with *being* rhythm. For many people the latter concept might seem tantamount to relearning how to speak, or walk. Or hear. The journey toward a confident yet flexible time sense is posed to you within these covers.

I've found that many musicians have developed a passive time sense (outer-directed, conducted, or metronome-led) in preference to an active time sense (from within—inner pulse). You are holding your guidebook to inner pulse. Both Andrew and I were fortunate to have studied with James Wimer, a master teacher of music/inner pulse, and much of that wisdom has generously been poured into this book. A.C. Lewis has offered to be your tour guide into your senses and mind, and a willing tourist is one who'll take up residence in that domain. I wish you Charisius's rhythmic ideal.

GORDON GOTTLIEB
Percussion faculty, Juilliard School
Regular guest, New York Philharmonic
Studio musician, Steely Dan
Lifetime participant, Imperio Serrano
escola de samba, Rio de Janeiro

Preface

The common belief about rhythm, that you either have it or you don't, just isn't true. With study and attention, anyone can improve their sense of rhythm.

As a percussionist and drummer, I've been on a lifelong quest to understand and master rhythm and polyrhythm. The seeds for this book were planted in the mid 1980s, in an era when drummers suddenly were competing with drum machines, and a new standard of rhythmic accuracy was being set for all instrumentalists. In New York at the time, the quest for rhythmic excellence took on an exciting immediacy; perfect pulse became the Holy Grail.

I began the quest in earnest, taking notes and tips from other musicians, friends, colleagues, conductors, and teachers. I had the good fortune to study for a few years with a particularly outstanding teacher, James Wimer, in his influential musicianship school.

More recently, after years of thinking about rhythm, teaching drumset, percussion, and rhythm seminars, and looking for but not finding a book about rhythm and how to improve it, I concluded that writing one myself could be both practical and fun.

This volume is written in four books, each with a different emphasis. The first discusses rhythmic terms and concepts, born of necessity. When I found myself writing on the subject, I had to ask and answer for myself the tough question: What is rhythm, really? Book One is a dialogue on rhythm in the broadest sense. An in-depth understanding of rhythm concepts can deepen and inspire performance.

The second book suggests practical courses of study to develop and strengthen rhythm and pulse. It includes a comprehensive series of metronome exercises, a short course on hand drumming, and other ideas to improve and develop your rhythmic confidence and clarity of expression.

The third book addresses more advanced rhythms, including polyrhythms. It offers guidance for improving reading, understanding, fluency, and performance, and provides a course of study specifically for drumset players.

The fourth book considers human factors, such as nervousness, attitude, and performance habits, that can affect a musical career. It suggests extramusical areas of study that can influence one's rhythm, including language, history, and mathematics. All these factors can influence performance, and can make the difference between one performance, or performer, and another.

The purpose of the entire volume is to look at rhythm as comprehensively as possible. While some of the subject matter may seem tangential, the best musicians I know took all of it into consideration in one way or another, and continued to do so throughout their careers.

While rhythmic demands are often highest for drummers and percussionists, this book is intended for all musicians. There is material here for beginning to advanced to lifelong players. Some material may be familiar to more accomplished musicians, and some material may be difficult for beginners, but any player should find useful material.

I hope this book will help you in your own rhythmic quest.

ANDREW C. LEWIS
March, 2005

BOOK

1

What Is Rhythm?

What Is Rhythm?

Rhythm is the language of time.

The word *rhythm* comes from the Latin *rhythmus* and the Greek *rhythmos,* both meaning *to flow.* Everything flows in rhythm through time. Everything we do—walking, talking, breathing, sleeping, working, and thinking—we do in rhythm as we flow through time. Events flowing and unfolding in time sculpt, shape, and divide time. Perceiving and naming these shapes and divisions creates the vocabulary for the language of time.

Any and every action shapes time in some way. These shapes of time can be long or short, can repeat or occur just once. While repetitive rhythms are easier to perceive, all events—marbles thrown across the floor, leaves rustling in the wind, even the birth and death of beings or civilizations—describe some rhythm. There's an infinite variety of actions and events, so there's an infinite variety of rhythms. There is one in particular we all share: the rhythm of our planet Earth as it flows, rotating and revolving around and around through space and time.

Rhythm is how we perceive and measure time. Humanity awoke to the awareness of the passing of time in the passing of days and seasons. Logically then, days and years have become the basis of the language of time.

Adding days together creates the weeks and months; adding seasons and years creates decades and centuries, then the ages, epochs, eras, and eons—ever-longer units and ever-slower rhythms of time.

Dividing days into segments creates the morning, noon, and night; the hours, minutes, and seconds; the milli-, micro-, nano-, pico-, femto-, and attoseconds—ever shorter, smaller, infinitely faster units and rhythms of time.

Steady repetitive rhythms like these are called *periodic rhythms.* Anything that happens over and over at a consistent rate creates a periodic rhythm. Periodic rhythms, *repetitive patterns,* are basic to the world as we know it; they're the structure, the temporal foundation, the building blocks of the universe—the way the universe works.

Just as there are periodic rhythms, so are there *nonperiodic rhythms*—rhythms that do not repeat over and over again. A rhythm can happen just once, and that's it. Nonperiodic rhythms, instead of having to do with structure, usually occur when something falls apart. The marbles thrown across the floor create a unique rhythm once, and never again. That's called a *rhythmic gesture*. Very slow rhythmic gestures are difficult to discern. A boulder sitting in a field, created and dissolving at an imperceptible rate, is a very slow rhythmic gesture.

Some rhythms, like opening a door, signing your name, switching a light, or starting a car, repeat, but not exactly, and not in exact increments of time. They are repetitive, but not periodic; they don't describe a *pulse*.

Periodic rhythms, repetitive nonperiodic rhythms, and rhythmic gestures are the three families of rhythms.

We perceive and measure time with rhythm. Repetitive rhythms create units of time, which we use as standards, as markers, for measuring time. We generally speak about time in terms of units of various types. Any number of different kinds of time units—whether seconds, eons, moments, or generations—can be used for measuring time, like so many time rulers, each with a different standard of measurement. There are potentially infinite varieties of time rulers, from precisely exact to approximate and uncertain, but they all share one reference point: the present.

Except for *orbit, rotation,* and *revolution,* the terms describing the structural rhythmic foundations of the universe also describe the foundations of music. They are *cycle, wave, resonance, oscillation, beat, pulse,* and *frequency*.

Musicians make rhythms with musical instruments. That, you could say for our purposes, is music.

A musician's role is to perceive and measure time. We consciously feel, shape, divide, and *compose* time, to convey feeling.

Humans have been endowed with a *sense of rhythm,* which allows us to sense and speak the language of time, to appreciate rhythm in all its forms, musical and otherwise.

Sense of Rhythm

Sense of rhythm is the ability to perceive and measure time. Everyone is born with an innate sense of rhythm, beginning with the sensation of the heart beating in the womb.

The ability to musically feel and express rhythm is a talent like any other—some do so more easily than others, but everyone with a career in music devotes a great deal of time and attention to it. With practice, attention, and an open mind, rhythm improves.

Usually, "sense of rhythm" refers specifically to the ability to maintain a strong pulse, the most important aspect of a musical sense of rhythm.

A musician's job is to play sounds in time, so it stands to reason that the deeper a musician understands what rhythm and time are, the better his sense of rhythm can be.

Time

Time is a never-ending continuum of the ever-changing present. It's the medium in which rhythm occurs.

In music, *time* usually means the underlying periodic rhythm.

The *time* can refer to the meter or time signature, as in *this piece is in 3/4 time.*

Good time means rhythm with a steady pulse, as created by a clock, a metronome, or a good drummer.

A *good sense of time* usually means the relative ability to discern and maintain a steady pulse, as does *keeping good time.*

Sense of time, besides meaning a feeling for rhythm and pulse, also refers to keeping track of clock time, knowing what time it is. Musicians need also this sense of time. You can't be late for gigs. A musician likes to be *on time,* in every way.

Pattern

Pattern is a term for a recognizable arrangement of material, energy, time, or thought. While it can be singular, as in the pattern of the surface of a rock, it usually implies repetition of form. The universe is organized and unfolds in patterns.

Physical objects are patterns of shape, color, consistency, mass, and texture. Actions occur in patterns of motion; language in patterns of letters, words, and thoughts; history in patterns of development; and music in patterns of sound. Most of the terms discussed in this book describe patterns.

There's an infinite variety of patterns. A significant one is the manner in which our civilization has organized time.

After noticing time passing in units of days, we needed a system to synchronize ourselves with each other, so we created calendars and "clock time." Notably, with the exception of days per week, we divided time into multiples and divisors of the musically rhythmic number 12. The year is organized into 12 months, 4 seasons of 3 months each or 4 times 3. The day has 24 hours, organized into two 12-hour cycles, the first of which is divided into morning, afternoon, and evening—3 periods of about 4 hours each, or 3 times 4. Each hour has 60 minutes, and each minute 60 seconds, both 5 times 12. (We agreed upon 60 minutes and seconds, one supposes, because of the 5 digits of each hand, or because 60 is easier to deal with than 36 or 48. While 36 [3 times 12] and 48 [4 times 12] may be simpler rhythmically and mathematically, they are harder to visualize, less "round.")

Twelve is also the magic number for musical resonance. Twos, threes, and fours, the divisors of 12, create the fundamental harmonic and polyrhythmic relationships (discussed in the section "The Relationship Between Polyrhythm and Harmony," page 1▪28). Sound resonates in twelves.

Just as our discussion of rhythm involves the large, slow patterns of time created by our planet's rotations and revolutions, so can we go in the direction of the smaller and smaller, into the time of the tiny, the world of atoms, photons, electrons, and beyond. Without getting deeply into physics, it's difficult to discern whether these are physical objects or energy, or both. In any case, these tiny objects also have their patterns of motion—patterns that are both similar to and different from those of nature's larger phenomena. The particles and energies of the universe—atomic particles, light, electricity, radio waves, sound waves, x-rays, and so forth—also move in repetitive patterns creating periodic rhythms, called vibrations, oscillations, cycles, pulses, frequencies, resonance, and waves. Energy or objects flow in these patterns until another object or energy disturbs the flow, the rhythmos, the rhythm.

What this has to do with music is that music is constructed with the same patterns as the physical universe. The terms above describing physics also describe music. The relationship between physics, mathematics, and music is interesting and beautiful. This book touches upon these relationships here and there, but for further study read more about it. Some resources are listed in the bibliography.

Pulse

Pulse is a fundamental pattern in both nature and music. Pulse, and one's inner pulse, is indispensable for the performance of music.

Any steady repetitive action creates a pulse. Unless obstructed, the pulse then moves outward through air, liquid, or space, in an expanding circular pattern away from the object engaged in the repetitive action.

While a pulse can be singular, as in a wave pulse, which is the force generated when a bomb goes off, we will consider pulse to be the sequence of pulses created by repetitive actions.

The heartbeat is the best example of pulse, and is the most intimate, as it is fundamental to life. The pumping of the heart moves a force of blood throughout the body. This force is what we refer to as the pulse. When you put your fingers on your wrist just below the thumb, you feel it.

In the context of heartbeat, various meanings of the word *pulse* are evident: (1) Each contraction of the heart is called a pulse, a singular noun. (2) The continuous succession of contractions that go on for life is called the pulse, another noun. (3) The action of the heart is *to pulse,* a verb: The heart pulses. (4) What you feel transmitted by the push of the blood throughout the whole body is also a pulse, a noun describing the force emitted by the heart. Four distinct but related meanings.

The pulsing of the heart is called the heart*beat.* The word *beat* is often interchangeable with the word *pulse.* Some other synonyms for pulse include *wave, throb, undulate, resonate,* and *vibrate,* depending on the circumstance.

Any succession of up and down, in and out, round and round, or expansion and contraction creates a pulse of some kind, sometimes obvious, sometimes subtle, sometimes perfectly in time, sometimes not. Earth rotating (night and day), the tides, your heart, pistons in an engine, turbines in water, water dripping, electric current, radio waves, blinking lights, car alarms, bouncing balls, and the once ubiquitous pendulums of clocks, all create pulse.

Breathing creates pulse, both singular and plural. Every breath out creates one pulse of air. And while we don't usually think of the lungs as pulsing, lungs contracting and expanding are in fact pulsing. Fish pulse with gills.

Another good example of a pulse is a pulsar, that celestial object that has been intriguing astronomers for some time now. A pulsar is a star that emits radiation (light or radio or some other kind of waves) in discrete bursts at exactly consistent intervals of time. Radiation emanating from one point of a revolving star reaches us in the form of a pulse, like a revolving searchlight that points at your face every time it goes around.

That, by the way, is one excellent way to experience a pulse. Just watch the revolving light of a lighthouse.

There's a nice correlation here between mathematics and music. In geometry it's a given that two points in space define a line. In music and nature, two points in time define a pulse.

The heartbeat, while not a very steady pulse by musical standards, remains the best metaphor for the importance of pulse in music. Just as the heartbeat gives life to living things, the pulse gives life to music. Look at the *Oxford English Dictionary* definition of *pulseless:* "Devoid of life, energy, or movement. Void of feeling. Motionless, lifeless." Such is music without pulse. That's why developing one's pulse is indispensable for musical performance. Pulse is the heart, the center, the life giver, the glue that holds music together. Feeling the same pulse is how musicians can play together. Pulse is necessary for music.

There are, of course, moments in music when pulse is not asked for: aleatoric pieces, ambient music, and fermatas, for example. Even then, one can think of pulse in the singular, a wave of energy that animates those moments, gives them life, like one long pulse-breath.

The metronome is a musical instrument that provides an even pulse, with reference numbers indicating the rate of pulse. It's an invaluable tool for working on pulse, looked at in Book Two.

It is no accident that the traditional metronome provides a pulse that is more or less within the rhythmic parameters of the human heart. It beats within the range of the heartbeat's rate, from about 40 beats per minute, the rate of an athlete at rest, to about 200 beats per minute, the uppermost heart rate. The range in which we feel a pulse is the range at which the human heart beats.

One aspect of our job as musicians is to perceive and measure time, to be able to discern and provide a steady pulse. The criterion for deciding which musician to hire is often who can keep the steadiest pulse. The way to gain that skill is to develop the inner pulse.

Inner Pulse

The sensation of pulse generated within one's own body and mind is the *inner pulse.* It's the inner timekeeper, an internal clock that resides in the imagination. The more you consider it, imagine it, and work on it, the more real it becomes. Inner pulse is the most important element for a musical sense of rhythm.

Period

Any specific amount of time can be called a *period.* The term usually refers to the amount of time it takes to complete one action. A period is a specified duration of time.

A good example is the period in school. It is a specific amount of time used to complete one class. Fourth or fifth period is for lunch, and you get to go home after seventh.

Periodic rhythm was discussed earlier. The period in periodic rhythm refers to the amount of time it takes to complete the one action that repeats over and over. In the example of the earth rotating on its axis creating days and nights, one complete rotation of the earth, 24 hours, is the period. Lunar periods are from one full moon to another. One solstice to another is another period, also called a year.

Historical time is described by periods, eras, epochs, and ages. These terms indicate time encompassing historical events or developments. In geology, four eras, Precambrian, Paleozoic, Mesozoic, and Cenozoic, are long, long units of time, describing stages of the Earth's development. These eras are then divided up by periods—for example, the Mesozoic contains the Triassic, the famous Jurassic, and then Cretaceous periods. The periods are further subdivided into epochs and are also described as ages, as in "the age of the dinosaur."

Personal histories come in periods, like Picasso's "blue period," or a "difficult period" of one's life. A civilization can have various eras, as in an "era of progress." All of these—eras, epochs, and ages—are different terms describing periods of historical time. They are approximate, inexact amounts of time, and do not describe periodic rhythms.

In music, a period is a pair of motivically related phrases, a specific musical "sentence" of 8 or 16 bars, balancing each other like two clauses in a compound sentence (16 bars sometimes being called a *double period*).

The next three terms, *cycle, frequency,* and *wave,* are defined by their periods.

Cycle

In matters of time, the word *cycle* is often interchangeable with *period,* but it is more specific. A cycle is always made up of periods, but you can have periods without cycles. A period can happen once, like a gesture, like the time it takes for a single action, era, or historical event. Picasso's "blue period" never came around again. But a cycle always occurs as a repetitive pattern; something keeps coming around again. Birth and death and birth and death mark the cycle of life. Spring, summer, fall, and winter repeating is the cycle of the seasons. The hands of a clock go around and around in cycles of seconds, minutes, and hours. An orbit is a cycle of revolutions. A washing machine has wash and spin cycles. Going around in circles is cyclical. Bicycles and motorcycles are so named because of the cyclical circular motion of the wheels and pedals, legs or pistons. The verb *to cycle* refers to riding one, or to go around and around, to repeat. A cycle refers to the motion of an object from here to there and back again, as long as it does it over and over.

The Greek and Latin roots *kyklos* and *cyclus* mean *circle.* A cycle is a pattern that goes around and around, over and over again and again.

Cycles are important in art and music. Series of poems and songs that are connected by one theme or one hero are called cycles, like Franz Schubert's song cycles and Richard Wagner's *Ring* cycle. When all the symphonies of a particular composer are played in one series, it's called a cycle.

Most important for our purposes is the phrase *cycles per second.* If something cycles somewhere between about 16 and 16,000 times in a second it creates a sound wave, which we can hear. This particular kind of *wave* is what we use to create music, and is also called a *frequency* or a *pitch.* These three terms are discussed next.

Frequency

Frequency refers to the number of times one event occurs in a specific period of time.

Frequencies range from extremely slow to extremely fast, from the frequency of the birth of galaxies to the frequency of photons hitting your retina from a stream of light. When discussing frequency or cycles, the word *per* is used. Some well-known frequencies include 12 months per year, 7 days per week, and 24 hours per day. Sixty is the frequency of both minutes per hour and seconds per minute. There are 1,000 milliseconds per second, so 1,000 is the frequency of milliseconds per second. There is always a number associated with or implied by a frequency.

Frequencies can be approximate. They can change, and average out. The frequency of the use of the word *frequency* per paragraph in this short passage is approximately three and three-fourths. The frequency of trips to work for most people is once per day or five times per week, but it changes. The frequency of phone calls you make per day can vary from zero to hundreds, depending on what you do. The frequency of your study depends on how serious you are.

Frequencies are the essence of music. A pulse occurs at a steady frequency. Musicians spend their lives concerning themselves with the frequencies that occur per minute and per second, in ranges from about 30 per minute to about 16,000 per second. That's only about 16,030 frequencies. What's the big deal?

In music, when the frequency is per minute, it is called beats per minute (bpm), and it defines the *tempo*. When the frequency is per second, it is called cycles per second, and it defines the *pitch*. In music the word *frequency* is often interchangeable with the word *pitch*. Two important reference frequencies in music are (1) half seconds—that is, 120 beats per minute, also called *march time*, and (2) 440 cycles per second, which is the pitch A-440 used for tuning.

The slower frequencies—years, days, minutes, and seconds—are perceived as increments of time. As frequencies get faster, above about 300 per minute, when they're too fast to be discernible as subdivisions of time, they're perceived as tones or pitches, as sound waves. As the frequencies go up and up, they get higher and higher, until at above about 16,000 per second or so they become too fast for us to hear. We know they exist, as supersonic waves, radio waves, ultraviolet waves, x-rays, and other waves, with light waves being the fastest. Waves are all over the place, and *wave* is the next term to deal with.

Wave

A wave is a pattern of motion, of traveling energy. It is energy flowing through a medium. An object moving in any medium creates a wave.

Like pulse, *wave* can be singular or plural. A single wave is the result of one impulse or action. As mentioned discussing pulse, a wave pulse is the energy that goes out when a bomb explodes. That energy, the pulse, moves in the form of a wave. As such, *wave* indicates a swelling and subsequent subsiding, as in a crime wave or wave of emotion. Our discussion, though, is about continuous repeating waves, just as it is more about continuous pulses.

There are a few ways to visualize moving waves. A snapshot of perfectly even waves seen from the side traveling on the surface of water could look like this familiar pattern, also called a *sine wave:*

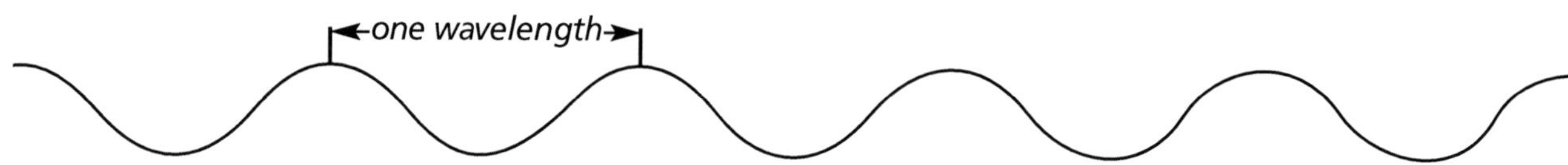

The topmost point is called the *peak*, and the bottommost point is called the *trough*. All waves have frequencies, which are their particular rhythm, or pulse. The frequency of a wave refers to the number of times the peak arrives at a given point in any given period of time.

The distance from peak to peak is called the *wavelength*. The characteristics of a wave are determined by their wavelength, their frequency, and the shape of the wave, called the *waveform,* which determines the timbre.

Waves travel out in a circular pattern from their source through the surrounding medium. Radio waves transmitted from a tower are often drawn like this:

Any object moving in a cyclical pattern—that is, anything vibrating, pulsing, oscillating, or revolving—creates waves, and the waves move out through the surrounding medium at the same frequency as the motion of that object. (Hypothetically, if there is no medium surrounding the moving object, if it is in a vacuum, no wave is created.) The waves travel away in all directions from the object that created them, through the surrounding medium, until the waves are blocked or dispersed, or until they dissipate due to gravity or friction. A wave can be worn down or change directions, but the frequency doesn't change. The wave just gets weaker and weaker and finally peters out.

Waves can per seen, felt, or heard, depending on both their waveform and frequency, and depending on the medium through which they are traveling. Sound waves, waves that can be heard, travel easily through air and water, and with some difficulty through solids. A great way to see how waves work in various mediums is to hold rope or twine suspending a gong, hit the gong, and put it in water. When you hit it, the gong vibrates. You hear it by virtue of the waves traveling away from the resonating gong through the medium of air. You feel it from the waves traveling through the medium of the rope from which the gong is suspended. And when you put it in water, you see waves created by the gong traveling through the medium of water. It keeps vibrating, creating waves, until the friction of the air and water wear it down, fading away until it stops entirely.

The pitch of the wave goes down when you put the gong into the water, not because of the change in the medium in which the wave is traveling, but because the gong itself vibrates more slowly in the water.

The gong vibrates in what is called a *standing wave.* All musical instruments work using standing waves. A string or a reed vibrating is a standing wave. These standing waves then transmit energy out into the surrounding medium, creating sound waves flowing through the air. (There is that flow again, the *rhythmos,* the rhythm.) Creating waves is what music is all about. The musician's job, at its most basic, is to create sound waves. We're wave makers, and our job is to create waves at precise frequencies.

There are some waves that don't work quite the same way. These are the waves of subatomic particles—light waves, electromagnetic waves. As mentioned in the section about patterns, in the world of the super tiny, it is difficult to distinguish whether things are particles or waves, or both. Light consists of what seem to be little packets of energy, photons, moving through space as waves. These waves don't exist only by virtue of passing through a medium; they are like mediums unto themselves. They affect other subatomic particles when they crash into them, like pellets crashing into a wall, and they also act like other waves when they flow through space. But they are different from sound waves, which have no essence themselves. Sound waves are air molecules waving as the sound flows through the air. There are no "sound particles." On the other hand, photons, light waves, *are* light particles, flowing as waves through space. They themselves *are* the medium, and they also flow *through* a medium. That's why light waves travel through "empty" space, and sound doesn't.

Electrons and other subatomic particles have properties like standing waves. They vibrate at certain frequencies, like vibrating strings or reeds, locked into a tiny orbit. And they act like particles. In the subatomic world, objects are like tiny packets of energy resonating as standing waves. If you were small enough, you perhaps could hear their sound. An atom is made of standing waves in subatomic harmony. Sounds interesting.

Pitch

What we call a *pitch* is a wave occurring at one continuous frequency in the audible range, between about 16 and 16,000 cycles per second. A pitch is produced when any object vibrates, oscillates, cycles, or pulsates within this frequency range. This object, whatever it may be, constitutes a *pitch source.* All musical instruments are pitch sources, except nonpitched percussion instruments, and even their "nonpitched" sound consists of many pitches all mixed up.

Pitches are also referred to as *notes, tones,* and *frequencies.*

Western musical tradition has chosen a series of 12 pitches, based on their harmonic relationship, to be given the names A, A#/B♭, B, C, C#/D♭, D, D#/E♭, E, F, F#/G♭, G, G#/A♭, and their octave doublings—the familiar 12 pitches used in Western music. There's the magic 12 again. Out of a potential of about 16,000 pitches, only about 88, from the lowest note of the piano to the highest, have specific names. (Some instruments go just a bit further.) We only concern ourselves with 88 out of about 16,000 possible pitches. Much more manageable.

It's a mystery how the standard tuning frequency of A-natural was determined, but the accepted standard is now A-440, or 440 cycles per second. Questions have arisen about this pitch standard, because A-natural has been rising over the last few centuries, and in the past the standard was both less standardized and lower—about three-quarters of a step lower in Bach's day. The reference pitch, and so performance pitch, continues to rise. One theory holds that this is due to the tendency among many orchestra musicians to play a tiny bit sharp in order to differentiate their sound from those around them. Another theory holds that everything in human experience is getting faster, including pitch. Many orchestras tune to an A-442 or A-444. Some pre-tuned instruments, such as some vibraphones, are now tuned to A-442 or 444. In any case, for our purposes let's just agree that the standard is A-440.

If this is a book on rhythm, you may ask, why are we talking about pitch? The answer is that pitch is a very fast periodic rhythm, another form of pulse.

The Relationship Between Pulse and Pitch

Pulse and pitch are two aspects of the same phenomenon, that of frequency—slower frequencies are pulse, faster ones are pitch. We hear a pulse if something sounds at a frequency between about 30 to 300 times per minute. We hear a pitch if something sounds between about 16 and 16,000 times per second. The difference between pulse and pitch is one of relative frequency. A pitch is a pulse so fast that it is perceived as one continuous sound.

Consider double reeds vibrating one against the other. If you imagine the action in slow motion, you can visualize the reeds bouncing off each other. Each time they hit creates a sound, and it is the repetition of that sound that creates the pitch. Listen to that low A on a contrabassoon: you can almost hear the reeds bouncing off each other, flapping in the breeze.

Consider a bee. The flapping of its wings sounds to us like a "bzzzzz," an indefinite buzzy pitch, but a pitch nonetheless. To the bee itself, the wings flap, or pulse. Both we and the bee are right.

By virtue of this relationship, sharpness and rushing, as well as flatness and dragging, become conceptually interchangeable. One can be a metaphor for the other. To speed up is to go sharp, while to drag is to go flat. Similarly, when you play sharp, you're rushing, and if you're flat, it's a drag. Musicians strive to sharpen their sensitivity to both intonation and tempo at the same time. One common phenomenon in auditions and musical performance is called pushing, a result of trying too hard. An effect of pushing is to play too fast, to rush, and to play or sing sharp. The tendency to play fast is related to the tendency to play sharp.

Expanding on this metaphor, think of pulses as pitches. They are, mathematically and physically.

An A-natural one octave above A-440 has a frequency of 880 cycles per second. The A two octaves up vibrates at 1,760 cycles per second, and the next one is the highest A-natural on a piano, vibrating 3,520 times per second. Continuing this upward progression beyond the highest notes of the piano, we encounter the higher and higher A-naturals, at 7,040 and then 14,080 cycles per second, which many people cannot hear. The next A, A-28,160, is so high no one can hear it. It's still a pitch, but it's a *supersonic* pitch; we can't hear it, but a dog can. Pitches continue up in an infinite progression; we just call them something else.

Now go down, starting with A-440. If the frequency is halved, you arrive at A-220, an A-natural one octave lower. Continuing down by octaves, A-naturals occur at frequencies of 110, 55, and 27.5, the lowest note on a piano, and the lowest note of a contrabassoon using an extension. This low you can almost hear the two reeds flapping in the breeze. A tuba can go just a little lower than this, depending on the circumstance, but it is not a very clear pitch.

Continuing to descend you go down through the range of the intersection between pulse and pitch. The octave below the lowest note on the piano is a low A-natural at 13.75 cycles per second. While barely discernible as a pitch, like a buzz, it also sounds like a very fast pulse, a pulse at 825 beats per minute. This A is too low to be useful as a pitch, and a bit too fast to be used as pulse; it is in the range of the intersection between pulse and pitch.

The A below is way too low, six octaves below; it's 6.875 beats per second. Seven octaves below A-440, we find A-3.4375, also known as metronome mark 206, a *presto,* about the fastest setting for an old-fashioned metronome.

Continuing down by octaves, you encounter an *andante* A at 1.7185 and a *largo* A at .859375 cycles per second, metronome marks 103 and 51.5 respectively. A-naturals you can dance to.

Next comes the A down at .4296875 cycles per second. This A is the lowest one that we can still feel as a pulse. It's off the chart, at 25.8 beats per minute. This is the range at which pulse begins to feel like periods of time, the slow range in which we cannot perceive frequency as pulse anymore. Below A-.4296875, below metronome mark 25, pulse still exists; it's just that we lose the ability to keep track of it without timekeeping instruments. Pulse becomes a slow periodic rhythm.

The slower you can feel and play a pulse, the better your time. If you can keep a steady pulse below mm=25, terrific. Below mm=15, if you can keep a pulse every four seconds without subdividing, you're a master.

Continuing down off the chart, we encounter A-naturals at 12.9, 6.45, and 3.2, 1.6, .8, .4, and .2 beats per minute. That's an A-natural pulsing every half a minute!

Keep going down, imagining A-naturals at one pulse per minute, then every 2 minutes, every 4, 8, 16, and 32 minutes, down by octaves to every hour, 2 hours, 4, 8, and 16 hours, down to one pulse every 32 hours, longer than a day.

The Pythagoreans imagined what they called the "music of the spheres," that is, the musical harmony created by the resonance of the heavenly bodies. It would consist of pitches down in this range, and slower. How big would you have to be to actually hear the music of the spheres? It exists.

A way to tangibly experience the relationship between pulse and pitch is to perform an experiment with a couple of tape recorders. They have to be able to record and play back at both half and normal speed.

Record a pulse at half speed, and then play it back at regular speed. It will sound twice as fast. Record that faster pulse onto another tape recorder going half speed, and then play that back at normal speed, doubling up the pulse again. This is taking the pulse up by octaves. If you continue this progression, you will soon hear a low buzzy pitch. Keep doing this, and the pitch will keep going up by octaves. Make sure you start with a pulse having a duration of several minutes, or else there will not be much sound to hear as the pitch goes up. You will be shortening the duration of the pulse or pitch in half every time you jump an octave.

This experiment also illustrates the principle of timbre. If you use different sounds to play the same pulse, the same pitches will result, but they will sound quite different. If you use a legato low drum, the resulting pitch might have a smooth sound. If you clap, the same pitch will sound bright and edgy. If you sing short tones as a pulse, the same pitch will have an entirely different sound. Different materials pulsing create different-sounding pitches.

Where there's a pulse, there's a pitch, and vice versa.

Beat

Beat has meanings in both music and in everyday language. For example, it can mean *to hit*. You can beat a dead horse, a dirty rug, or a drum. All can produce a musical beat, which is an audible succession of beats. A beat can be singular or plural. One sound produced on a drum is one beat, as is a series of sounds in rhythm from the same drum.

Beat usually refers to organized pulse, a particular rhythm. Drummers play beats, or *drumbeats,* rhythmic patterns. To *keep a beat* is to maintain a rhythm.

Beating can also refer to something moving back and forth, like wings beating. This kind of beating creates waves and pulses.

A particular beat can identify a style of music or dance, like a jazz, rock, or swing beat.

A *beat pattern* is the hand motion a conductor uses to communicate meter to the orchestra; each change of direction communicates a beat. The *downbeat* is the first beat in each bar or measure of music. See page 4▪19.

Groove

To *groove* is to pulse in a swinging way, to play in time with a good "feel." When you're *in the groove,* you stay right there like the needle in the groove of an old LP. It's a metaphor for rockin', solid, swingin', flowing time.

Tempo

The *tempo* is the speed at which a piece is or should be played. To *keep the tempo* means the rhythm doesn't get faster or slower.

The term *a tempo* means return to the tempo you started with, or take the music at the correct tempo. The numbers on a metronome provide the standard reference for tempos.

Rushing and Dragging

These are terms describing the act of changing the tempo during performance. To rush is to get faster, to push or hurry, and to drag is to get slower, to drag the tempo back.

You can rush or drag notes by playing them early or late, without actually speeding up or slowing down the underlying tempo.

Meter and Time Signature

Meter is the organization of pulse. It's the grouping of beats into musical form. The meter is defined by the time signature. For that reason meter is often referred to as the "kind of time" being used.

The *time signature* indicates the meter, defined by the two numbers placed at the beginning of written music. While it looks a bit like a fraction, in that it is written with one number above another, it is not. The upper number indicates how many beats per bar or measure, and the lower number indicates the kind of note that is used as one beat—that is, whether the quarter note, half note, eighth, or 16th, determines the basic pulse of the music.

EXAMPLE 1.1

$\begin{smallmatrix}4\\4\end{smallmatrix}$ or $\begin{smallmatrix}3\\8\end{smallmatrix}$ or $\begin{smallmatrix}6\\2\end{smallmatrix}$ or $\begin{smallmatrix}9\\16\end{smallmatrix}$ or $\begin{smallmatrix}8\\8\end{smallmatrix}$ ← Number of beats per measure / ← Kind of note that gets the beat

In written music, *bar* and *measure* mean the same thing. It is one unit of the beats indicated by the time signature, and is delineated by "bar lines" at the beginning and the end.

Regular meter is either in duple (two beats per measure), triple (three beats per measure), or quadruple (four beats per measure). *Irregular meters,* also called *odd time signatures,* organize time into. 5's, 7's, 10's, 11's, and so on. Odd times are combinations of duple, triple, and quadruple time, "added together" in each bar. *Multimeter* is the term for music that changes meter in quick succession, also called *alternating meter.*

Meter can be simple or compound. These terms refer to how each beat in the measure is naturally subdivided, and have nothing to do with the number of beats in a measure. There are two basic subdivisions of the beat, into two and into three. *Simple meters* divide each beat into two, and *compound meters* divide each beat into three. Compound meters use dotted notes as their basic beats, and so the basic beats have values of three. (A dotted note adds half the value of the note to the same note, so a dotted quarter note has the value of a quarter plus half a quarter, for a total of three eighths. A dotted half has the value of three quarters, and a dotted whole note has the value of three half notes.)

You can also look at compound time or compound meters as those created by multiplying simple meters by three, creating compound duple (6/2, 6/4, 6/8), compound triple (9/4, 9/8, 9/16), and compound quadruple meters (12/4, 12/8, 12/16). I find that more confusing, and so prefer to think of compound meters simply as those built on dotted notes, or again, as meters in which the basic beats are divided by three.

2/4, 3/4, and 4/4 are simple meters because each beat, the quarter note, is naturally subdivided into two eighths. 3/8 also is simple, because the basic beat, an eighth note, is naturally subdivided into two 16th notes. But at a fast tempo, 3/8 can also be considered compound. 6/8, 9/8, and 12/8 are compound meters, with each beat organized into three eighths. 6/4, 9/4, and 12/4 are compound if the tempo goes fast enough for every three quarter notes to be organized into pulses of dotted half notes.

Note that while the upper number in the time signature can be any number, the lower is always 2, 4, 8, 16, 32, or more rarely 64, and 1. That's because it refers to the *kind* of note that gets the beat, so the 2 stands for half note, the 4 stands for quarter note, the 16 stands for 16th note, and so on. (When you see 1 in the lower position, which occurs rarely, it stands for the whole note getting the beat.) There is no such thing as a third note, a fifth note, or a seventh note. Yes, a triplet comprises something resembling third notes, but we just don't write out time signatures that way. It becomes unnecessarily complicated.

So, you can have 27/8 time, or even fractions in the upper position, like 3½/4 time, but sadly you just can't have 4/3 time. You sometimes see an altered note in the lower position: a dotted note. You pronounce that time signature as "four over dotted quarter." But it really sounds like a 12/8.

There are a few shorthand conventions for calling out time signatures. *Common time* is another way to say 4/4, and *cut time* is another way to say 2/2. *Waltz time* is a three at a well-understood but imprecise tempo. *March time* is a standard, at mm=120; it's usually in cut time, but you can have 4/4 marches as well. Specific dances are associated with well-known times, such as *polka time* (a fast 2/4), *swing time,* and some others.

In written music, while the bar line indicates the fundamental organization of the pulse, there are other simultaneous organizations of the pulse. The main beats in the bar are subdivided by smaller beats, also called the *smaller note values,* which can be organized in groups independent of the main beats. You can consider and feel each bar line as a larger beat or pulse. The big pulses of downbeats are then organized into even larger pulses, of phrases and statements. There are other potential organizations of pulses—phrases that are not defined by the downbeats. Music has pulses within pulses within pulses. Meter is a basic organization of pulse, along with which there can be infinite smaller and larger organizations of pulse.

While the time signature of Western music gives enormous flexibility in organizing pulse, especially when we consider that we can change the time signature from bar to bar, it doesn't easily allow us to notate meter in many other styles of music in the world. In Latin music, the meter, the organization of pulse, is called the *clave.* The basic clave is an organization of 16 pulses grouped into three-three-four-two-four. In 4/4 time, you can have 3+2 clave or 2+3 clave.

EXAMPLE 1.2

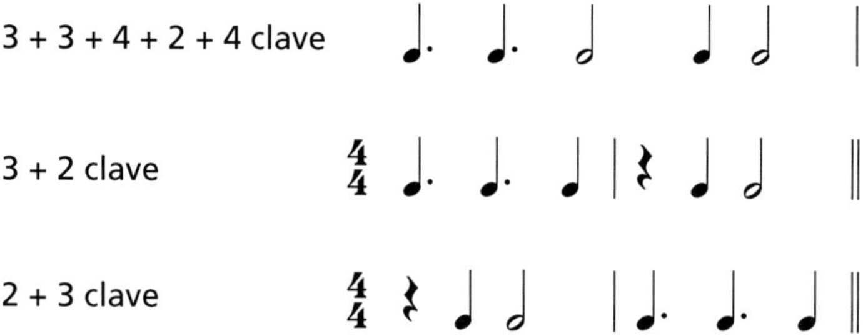

This can be notated, but the notation doesn't truly capture the organization of the pulse, the "feel."

Similarly, much of traditional music from India escapes written definition in our system. Ragas can be written, but the notation becomes complicated and fails to capture the essence of the style.

The time signature system is particularly inadequate in much African music, because African music is often organized by more than one basic pulse at a time. It is polymetric—not easily expressed by our notational system.

Polymeter

Polymeter occurs when there are two meters going on at the same time. A piece or section of a piece written in two meters is polymetric. In written music the polymeter is indicated by having two different time signatures.

Polymeter was an important aspect of Renaissance music (occurring in a period lasting roughly from 1400 to 1600). The following is an example from a motet by Guillaume Dufay (1399–1474), a well-known Renaissance composer:

EXAMPLE 1.3

It is written in 3/2 and 6/4. They both share the six beats, but they organize them differently. The top line divides the six beats into three groups of two quarters, and the second line organizes them into two groups of three quarters. The second beat of the two dotted half notes occurs precisely in between the second and third beat of the three halves, creating two independent but intimately related pulse phrases. This kind of organization—*three over two*, or *two over three*—is the most common and fundamental polymeter and is also called the *hemiola*. It looks like this:

EXAMPLE 1.4

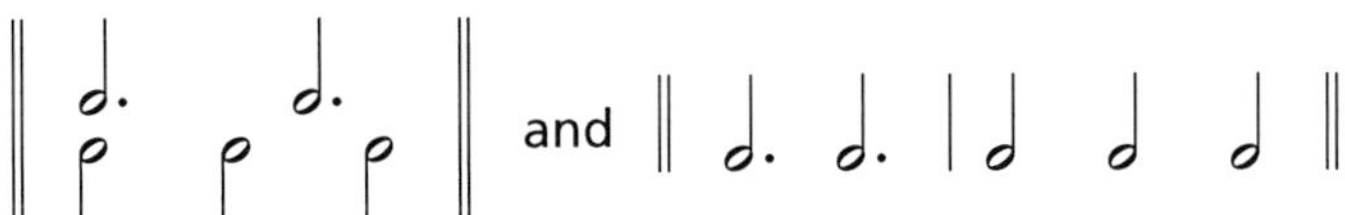

This style of rhythm, popular in the Renaissance, went out of fashion in written music and didn't come back into vogue until the 20th century. A rare example of polymeter occurring between the Renaissance and the 20th century is from Mozart's opera *Don Giovanni:*

EXAMPLE 1.5

A 3/8 over a 2/4 over a 3/4—a compound and two simples! The basic pulse stays the same, but the subdivision and the organization differ.

Mozart used polymeter here to support what was going on in the opera. There are three simultaneous time signatures for three simultaneous scenes, each with separate music and action going on.

Polymeter started creeping back into Western music around the beginning of the 20th century. Charles Ives (1874–1954) was a great proponent of polymeter. His fourth symphony requires two conductors for performance, to keep track of the simultaneous meters.

The previous examples are what are called *vertical polymeter.* That's when the two meters occur at the same time. *Horizontal polymeter,* a kind of alternating meter, occurs when music is written in two meters that keep switching back and forth, "taking turns." The song "America" from Leonard Bernstein's *West Side Story* is a perfect example:

EXAMPLE 1.6 "America" from Leonard Bernstein's *West Side Story*

This too is a kind of polymeter. Polymeter in written music is usually indicated by the time signature.

Polyrhythm

Polyrhythm generally refers to two rhythms of differing metrical structure occurring at the same time. It is sometimes known as *cross rhythms.*

In a sense, all music is polyrhythmic, in that you can find more than one rhythm in any piece of music. Even a very simple rhythm, such as a pattern of 12 quarter notes in 4/4 time, has the pulse of the quarter notes *and* the pulse of the downbeats.

EXAMPLE 1.7

The bar lines create an emphasis on each downbeat, creating a four over one, along with the implied rhythm of the subdivisions, the "hidden" eighths and 16ths. While these are different rhythmical structures, different organizations of pulses, they are not "counter" to each other, in that the basic organization of pulse is the same. Each bar remains firmly in 4/4, and each beat is subdivided by two or multiples of two.

To create a polyrhythm, you need phrases of two and three, or three and four, or four and five, and so on, at the same time. Two over four or four over eight don't count. If the rhythms going over each other are all powers of two (that is, 1, 2, 4, 8, 16, 32, or 64), there is no polyrhythm, in the strict sense.

Take the same three bars with 12 quarter notes in 4/4 time, and group every unit of three quarter notes together, as follows:

EXAMPLE 1.8

This creates the polyrhythm of four over three, or four groups over three bars. The beats are organized into groups of three, while the meter indicates to organize the beats into groups of four. When the beats "disobey" the metrical structure, or if subdivisions "disobey" the natural subdivision organization, creating a different pulse structure, polyrhythm happens.

Take the same number of quarter notes, and this time organize them in 3/4 time, grouping every four beats together, as follows:

EXAMPLE 1.9

This creates the polyrhythm of three groups over four bars—or three over four.

If the three bars of four quarter notes are played at the same time as the four bars of three quarter notes, it is a vertical polyrhythm. A horizontal polyrhythm occurs when the contrasting rhythms are played one after the other.

A good example of horizontal polyrhythm is the same one we used for polymeter, "America" from *West Side Story.*

Polyrhythms very often occur for just a moment, as in the example from Aaron Copland's *Rodeo* suite, called "Buckaroo's Holiday," on the following page. This piece is in 4/4, but for three bars Copland groups the timpani, tuba, and trombone in a polyrhythmic four over the three bars, while the winds and trumpets do not participate.

EXAMPLE 1.10 From "Hoe Down" in Aaron Copland's *Rodeo* suite:

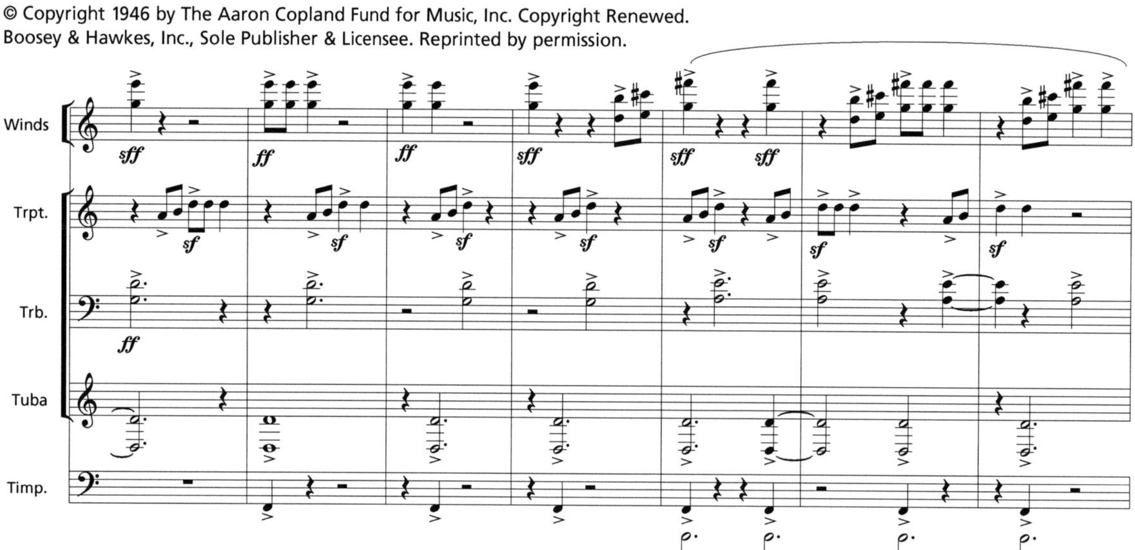

This moment from the *Rite of Spring*, by Igor Stravinsky (1882–1971), is a pinnacle of polyrhythm in Western concert music:

EXAMPLE 1.11

70

Fl. gr.

Cor. 1. 2.

Tr. picc. (Re)

ff con sord.

Tr. (Do) 2

con sord.

ff

Trb.

con sord.

fff

Tuba

ff

Timp.

Gr. C.

Tamtam

Une rape Guiro

etc. sim.

Bassi

ff

70

EXAMPLE 1.11 *(continued)*

There are so many different pulse structures occurring here at the same time. Over just these eight bars, you can find pulses grouped into units of 3, 4, 6, 8, 12, 16, 24, and 32. Also, in each bar there are smaller polyrhythms of 2 over 3 over 4 over 6. The chart on the next page shows all the pulse structures in this climactic moment.

Polyrhythm and polymeter are closely related terms. Polyrhythm is comprehensive; polymeter is one specific kind of polyrhythm. In order for a polyrhythm to be considered polymetric, it should be stated in the time signature, or it should go on for an entire piece, or at least for a long time. The Stravinsky quoted above could be considered polymetric if it went on longer, or if he had written a different time signature for some of the parts. But he didn't, so it's considered polyrhythmic, but not polymetric. The boundaries are sometimes blurred.

EXAMPLE 1.12 Polyrhythms in "Jeux de Cites Rivales" from Igor Stravinsky's *Rite of Spring:*

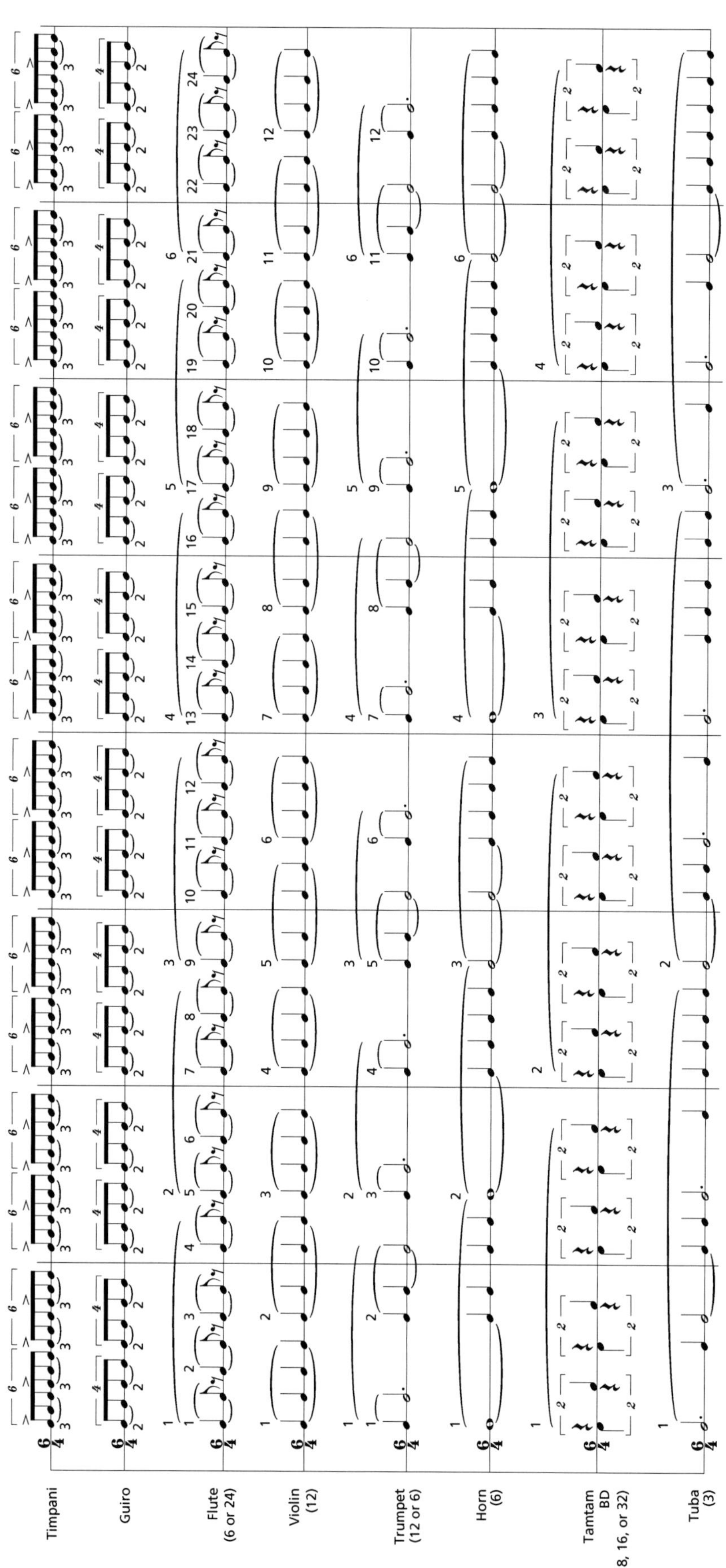

Polyrhythms in these eight bars: 3 over 4 over 6 over 8 over 12 over 16 over 24 over 32.

Polyrhythms in each bar: 2 over 3 over 4 over 6.

Hemiola

The hemiola is a special and specific foundation in music. The word comes from the Latin roots *hemi* and *holos,* meaning half and whole.

Hemiola originally had to do with halves and wholes. Here is some musical math: Two halves make a whole, as in two half notes make a whole note. Three halves make another kind of whole, a set or unit of three, as in a dotted whole note. Two groups of the unit of three make another kind of whole, a unit of six. Three groups of the unit of two also make a "whole" of the same six beats. Six can be divided up two ways, as three half notes or two dotted half notes, three and two.

EXAMPLE 1.13

Six beats can be evenly divided the following ways:

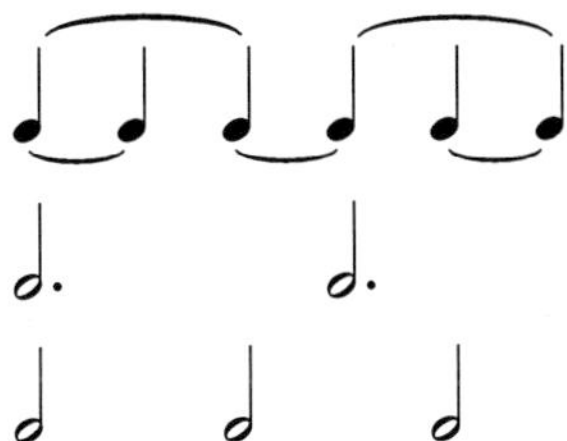

I know it's a bit strange; there is more than one kind of "whole" going on here.

This demonstrates the original rhythmic meaning of hemiola: six beats divided into three groups of two and two groups of three, alternating back and forth, three over two. The ratio of three over two is the classic hemiola.

Two over three—and the mirror image three over two—is the most fundamental polyrhythmic relationship, and the most fundamental harmonic relationship. The term originally had both rhythmic and harmonic meanings. The ratio of three over two is the relationship of a perfect fifth. But I'm getting ahead of myself.

During the Renaissance era, the hemiola of three groups of two over two groups of three was a standard compositional form, as seen in the Dufay excerpt in example 1.3.

The following are examples of hemiola from later periods. The first movement of Beethoven's Third Symphony is written in a fast 3/4, organized in units of three beats, as outlined in the opening statement, the cello melody:

EXAMPLE 1.14

There are two "halves," of three beats each, of a "whole" of six beats, made by two bars. By reorganizing the six beats into three half notes (two beats each), we obtain the hemiola. Beethoven uses this rhythmic relationship frequently in this piece, notably in the climax of the exposition, shown below. The silence on the strong beat of each half note creates a syncopated hemiola.

EXAMPLE 1.15

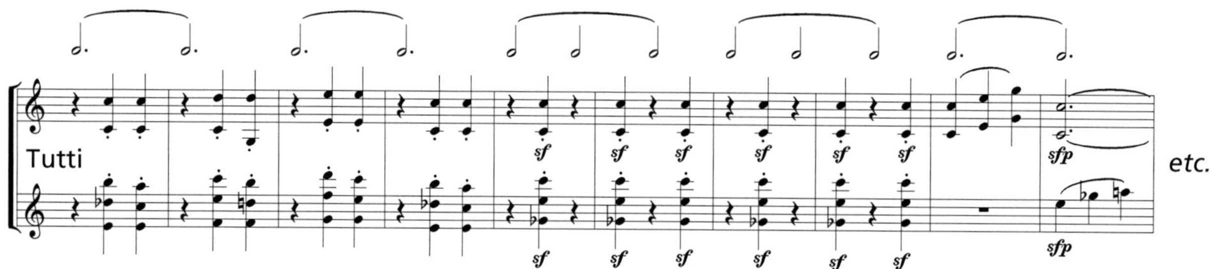

This example, and the piece, is polyrhythmic, but not polymetric. The piece remains firmly in 3/4 time.

The opening theme of Robert Schumann's third symphony, the *Rhenish,* is a hemiola right from the start. The meter is again in 3/4, but the melody is organized in units of two beats each, as shown in the violin line:

EXAMPLE 1.16

You could write out the opening in 2/4, a nice melody that way as well, and this is what it would look like.

EXAMPLE 1.17

In the following memorable hemiola moment from the last movement of Hector Berlioz's *Symphony Fantastique,* he rocks the three over two back and forth between two halves of the orchestra, within the fast 6/8, creating a polyrhythmic battle that baffles even the best orchestras.

EXAMPLE 1.18 From last movement of Berlioz's *Symphony Fantastique:*

Over time, hemiola began to be used to refer not just to groups of twos and threes but more generally to any rhythmic phrasing that occurs contrary to the stated meter. Phrasings of fours or fives in 3/4 time, or threes, fives, and sevens in 4/4 time, and so forth, are now called hemiolas. Hemiola can refer to almost any temporary polyrhythm.

Johannes Brahms (1833–1897) did not write polymetrically, but he often wrote polyrhythmically. He was a master of hemiolas, using them structurally and thematically. Look at this spot from the last movement of his Second Symphony, written in 4/4. In this section starting nine bars before letter F, he wrote hemiolas of four over five bars, and four over three bars, within the same phrase, with a fast three over two (the triplets) in the last bar:

EXAMPLE 1.19

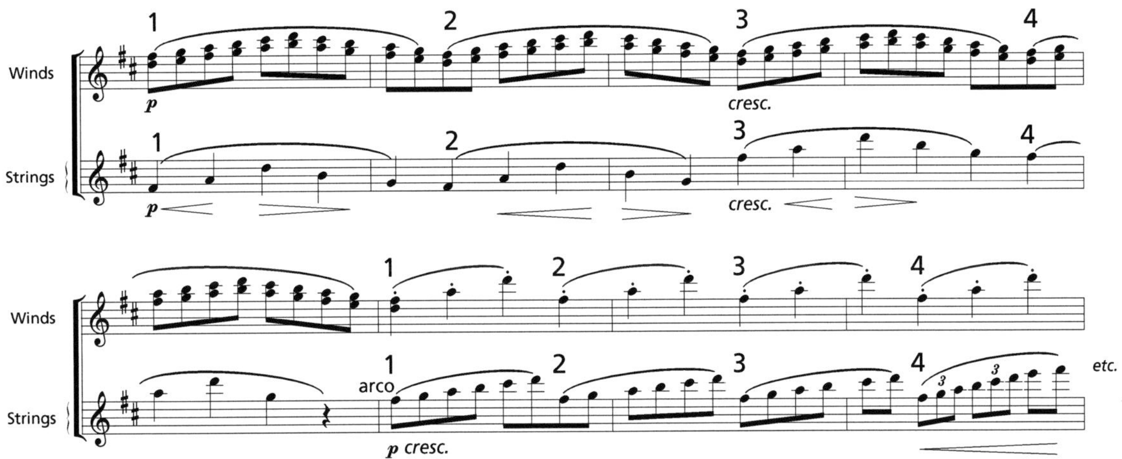

The Relationship Between Polyrhythm and Harmony

Harmony deals with relationships between pitches. The relationship between any two pitches, the difference in sound, creates a harmonic *interval.* This interval is perceived as the "distance" between the two pitches. Pitches, also called *frequencies,* have a numeric value, a number, which is the number of times the pitch source vibrates per second. The relationship between the frequencies' numbers creates the harmonic interval.

We discussed how a pitch is a frequency, and how a frequency is also a pulse, defined by the number of times something pulses or beats within a certain period of time. It follows that if a harmonic interval is the relationship between two pitches, it is also the relationship between two pulses, and the relationship between two numbers.

Originally, hemiola had a harmonic significance as well as a rhythmic significance. It referred to a specific interval, the perfect fifth. This is because if you look at any two pitches in a relationship of a perfect fifth, you discover a rhythmic relationship of two over three.

The following spells it out using frequency numbers for pitches.

Start with the reference pitch A-440. This pitch resonates when something beats or cycles 440 times per second. The perfect fifth above it resonates at 660 cycles per second, a pitch we call E-660. Musicians identify E-660 as a perfect fifth higher than A-440. The harmonic distance between the two pitches is a perfect fifth. The numeric distance between the two frequencies is 220 cycles per second.

The A an octave below A-440 resonates at a rhythm of 220 cycles per second. The number 220 is one-half of 440, the relationship of two to one. 220 is a unit of one half of 440. It follows that two halves make a whole of 440, and three halves (*hemi* plus *ola*) make a whole of 660.

Two times 220 equals 440 (A-440). Three times 220 equals 660 (E-660). In this case, 440 is the whole, 220 is the half, and 660 is the whole plus half.

The relationship of the frequencies of 440 to 660 is the same relationship as two to three. $2 \times 220 = 440$. $3 \times 220 = 660$.

Look at an octave below A-440—that is, A-220. One half of 220 is 110. If you add 220 plus 110, you get 330. That note, E-330, is a perfect fifth above A-220. In this case, A-220 is the whole, A-110 is the half, and E-330 is the whole plus half. $2 \times 110 =$ A-220. $3 \times 110 =$ E-330. Two is to three as A is to E.

A "whole" of 660 consists of six times 110, three times 220, two times 330, or one and a half (*holos* plus *hemi*) times 440. There is a relationship between the pitches and the numbers, a relationship between music and math, and also a relationship between polyrhythm and harmony. Two over three equals a musical perfect fifth.

EXAMPLE 1.20 The relationship of all the A's and E's in the audible range:

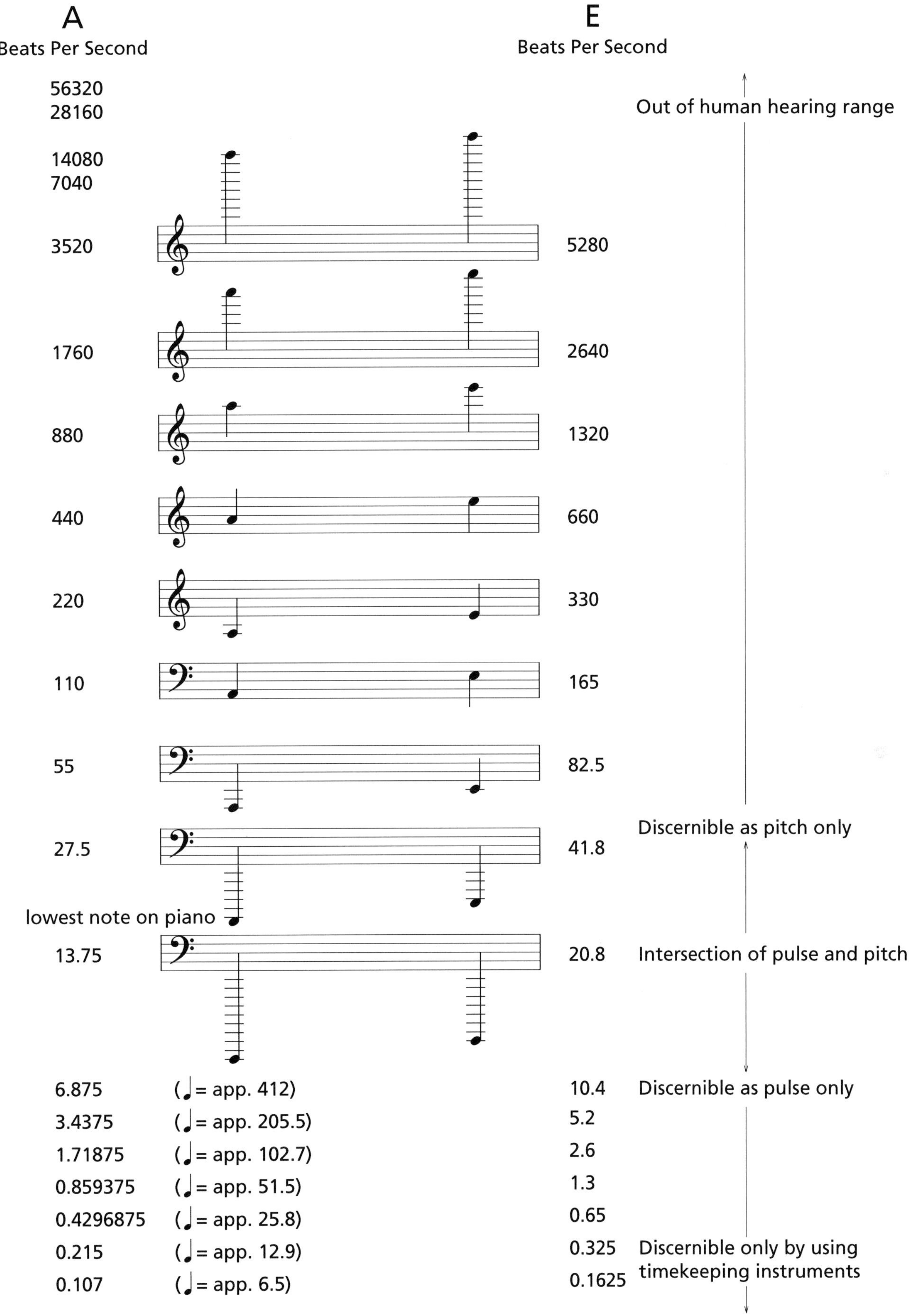

Here's an experiment to see and hear this. Take two tape recorders that can record on both the right and left channels separately, recorder A and recorder B. They must also be able to record at two speeds, one twice as fast as the other, as in the pulse-to-pitch experiment outlined earlier. We will call them half and normal speeds. You also need a pair of headphones.

Record a pulse on the left channel of recorder A going at half speed, a nice slow groove using just one tone. You need some patience to do this experiment, because you have to record the pulse for a long time. Record it for eight minutes.

EXAMPLE 1.21

mm half note = approx. 51.5; a low A-natural

Listen to the playback of that slow pulse in your headphones. Subdivide each half note you hear into quarter-note triplets, so that you are imagining this rhythm:

EXAMPLE 1.22

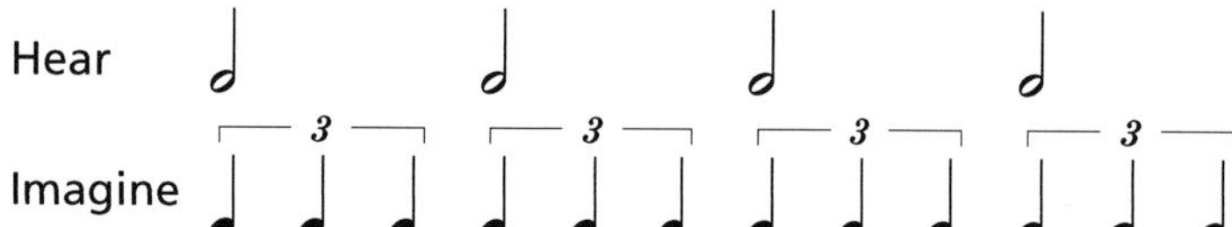

Now group those quarter-note triplets in units of two, as follows:

EXAMPLE 1.23

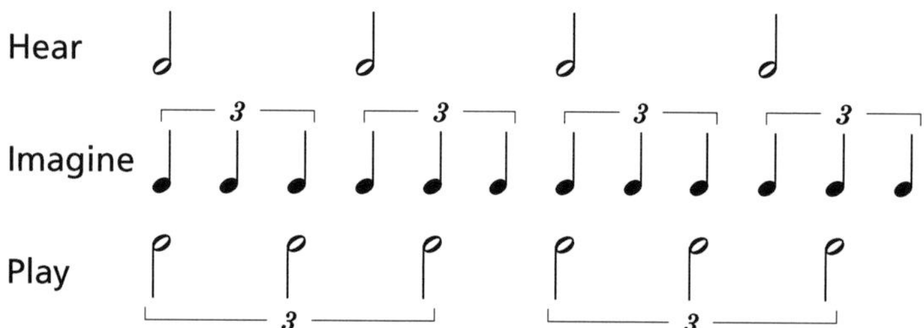

Now record this new pulse on the right channel of the same recorder A still going at half speed, as you listen to the original groove performed on the left channel.

EXAMPLE 1.24

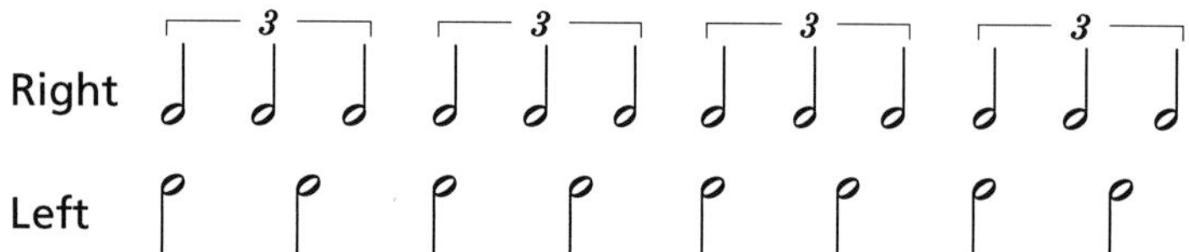

You are performing a three over two. Record this three over two for the full eight minutes.

Stop recording and listen back. The resulting rhythm is a classic hemiola:

The slower pulse is coming out of the left channel, and the faster pulse is coming out of the right channel of recorder A.

Now switch recorder A to play both channels twice as fast, at normal speed. The groove goes by twice as fast, the slower pulse still coming out of the left, the faster one out of the right. This will now take four minutes to play, one-half the time, one octave higher.

EXAMPLE 1.25

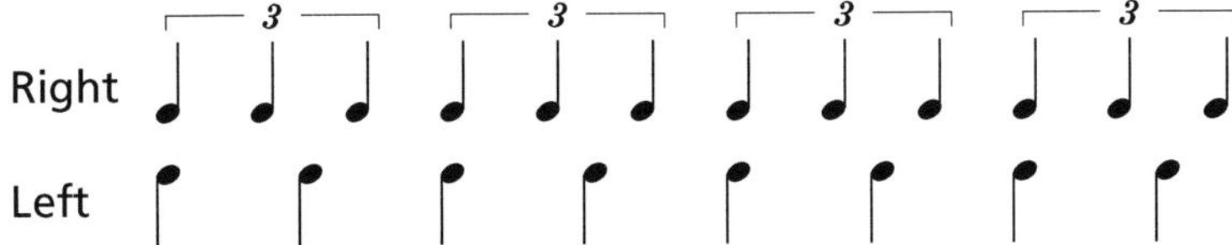

Record the sound coming out of the recorder A going at normal speed onto the recorder B going at half speed.

When done, switch recorder B to normal speed and play it back. You will hear the same polyrhythm going by twice as fast. The recording will now take two minutes to complete.

EXAMPLE 1.26

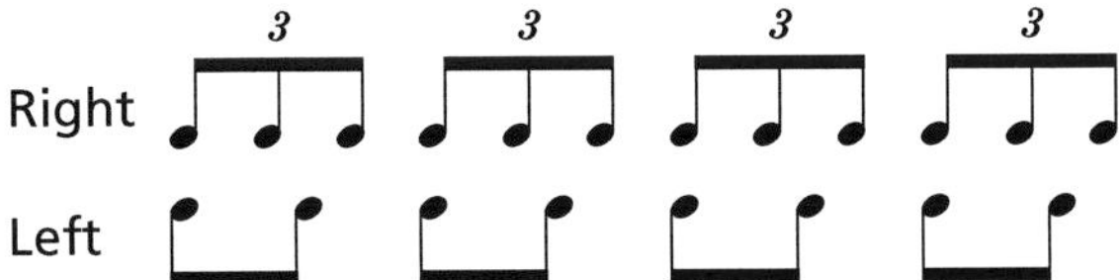

Record that onto recorder A going at half speed.

Repeat this process, switching the recorders so that you keep recording at half speed and playing back at normal speed. The recording length keeps halving, from one minute (mm=412) to 30 seconds (mm=824), then down to 15 seconds (mm=1,648). The sound keeps going up by octaves. Once you get the recording to go this fast, it will get too fast to hear pulses; you'll hear what sounds like pitches—buzzy, weird-sounding pitches. The harmonic interval of these two weird-sounding pitches will be a perfect fifth.

EXAMPLE 1.27

15 seconds

right channel E: 41.8
left channel A: 27.5

When the left channel is pulsing at 1,648 beats per minute, you're hearing what is also known as A-27.5, the lowest note on the piano.

One more way of seeing this relationship of the rhythmic perfect fifth is to do another "speeding up" process, recording the pulses one after the other, instead of at the same time. This will create a horizontal instead of a vertical hemiola, and a succession of perfect fifths, intervallic leaps, pitches coming one after the other.

Make a recording a full eight minutes long, alternating between one minute of the slower rhythm with one minute of the faster rhythm.

Both tracks have this rhythm:

EXAMPLE 1.28

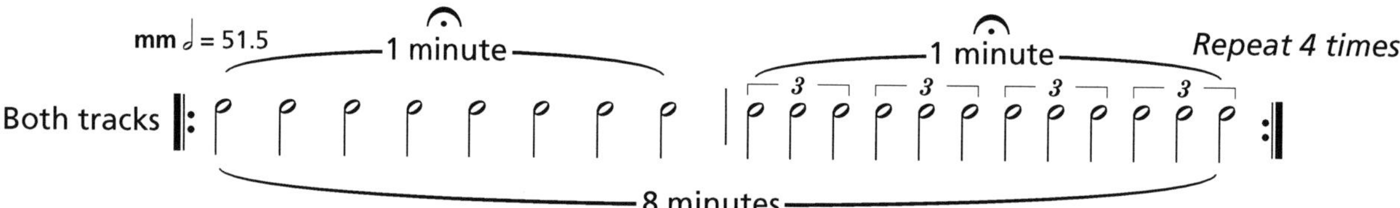

When you double the tape speed, the recording becomes four minutes long. Keep going up octaves by doubling the tempo a second time; the recording becomes two minutes long. A third time it becomes one minute; the fourth about 30 seconds. On this 30-second recording, you will hear a pitch going up and down by a perfect fifth, A to E, four times.

EXAMPLE 1.29

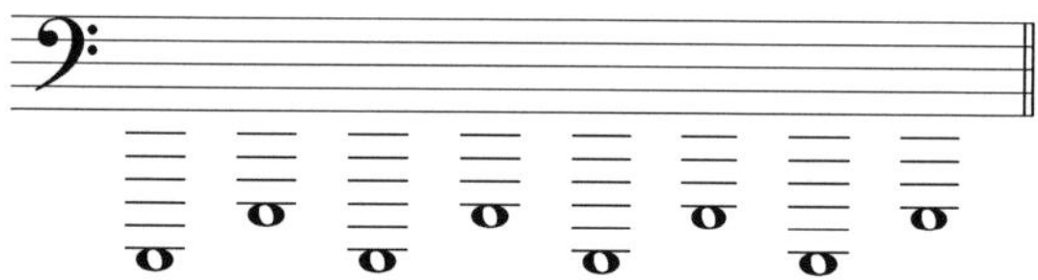

This concept does not pertain only to perfect fifths. Every interval has some polyrhythmic relationship. The harmonic relationship of a perfect fourth has the rhythmic relationship of four over three. If you perform the experiment with the recording device outlined above, but instead played the following two grooves on the left and right channels,

EXAMPLE 1.30

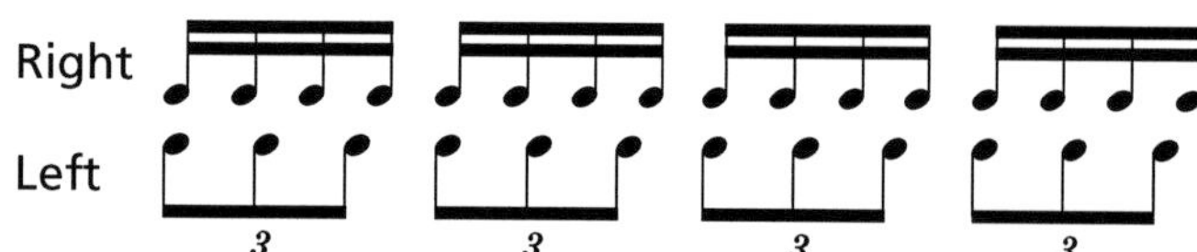

and then speed it up again and again as done in the previous experiment, the sound you'd finally hear would be a perfect fourth.

To look at a perfect fourth from a mathematical perspective, take the E-660. Play the octave above the A-440—the A-880. The harmonic relationship between E-660 and A0-880 is a perfect fourth. The polyrhythmic relationship between E-660 (3 × 220) and A-880 (4 × 220) is three over four.

The lowest common multiple of the numbers that create the relationship of fourths (four over three) and fifths (three over two) is 12. There's that 12 again. The relationships of these numbers are the relationships found in octaves, perfect fourths, and perfect fifths—the relationships of the tonic, the subdominant, and the dominant. Classical harmony is built on these rhythmic mathematical relationships, and they all come out of the subdivisions of 12. Twelve is the magic number for fundamental polyrhythmic music, and it is the magic number for the resonance of the tonic-dominant relationship. That's why I say, through luck or intuition, we organized clock time to musically resonant frequencies.

Every musical interval—from seconds to ninths and beyond—can be described in terms of some mathematical and rhythmic relationship.

It's not a stretch to say that polyrhythms are pulses that are in harmony with each other. Just as the relationship between pulse and pitch is one of relative frequency, so is the difference between polyrhythm and harmony. Every harmony has some rhythmic relationship. It's a nice way to think about it. When you are playing a chord, you are also playing a complex, super-fast, polyrhythmic groove.

Metric Modulation

Metric modulation refers to changing the basic pulse of a piece, to change the metronome mark, by using a polyrhythmic relationship between one section and another.

The simplest metric modulation is by octaves, which rhythmically means to either double the tempo (an octave up) or cut the tempo in half (an octave down).

If you modulate metrically by two over three or three over two, you are modulating by rhythmic fifths. The recording exercise above, example 1.28, shows a pulse modulating back and forth by fifths.

If you modulate by three over four, or four over three, then it's by fourths. The following short example from Elliott Carter's (b. 1908) *March* for solo timpani illustrates modulating rhythmically up a fourth.

EXAMPLE 1.31 "March" from *Eight Pieces for Four Timpani* by Elliott Carter

The metronome mark in the first bar is mm=105. In the succession of B's to E's in the first bar, each note is three 16ths, or a dotted eighth, long. The dotted eighth becomes the quarter-note pulse in the next bar, indicated by the figure written above the bar line. This change metrically modulates the quarter-note pulse up one fourth from mm=105 to mm=140.

Look at example 1.8 again. Grouping the quarter notes into units of three instead of units of four, you create a four over three, a relationship of a perfect fourth. If you take those three quarters, and make their value a new bar-line value—in other words, if you suddenly change from 4/4 to 3/4 without changing the metronome mark, you also modulate metrically up a big fourth.

The term *metric modulation* nicely describes that pulse relationships can be seen as harmonic relationships. Pulse can modulate, just as harmony modulates.

Accent

Accent is another word for emphasis: it brings your attention to something, it pulls something out of a texture. It can refer to a spice on food, or a splash of color on a painting. Perhaps an accent in spoken language is referred to in this way because when you speak a language you don't know very well, you tend to place emphasis where it doesn't usually belong, thus changing the texture, bringing attention to unusual articulation and accents.

In music, accent strictly refers to the symbol > or ^ placed above a note. This is an indication to stress a particular note, usually accomplished by playing the note louder than the others. The accent indicated by this mark can also be accomplished by means other than dynamics—for example, by putting more weight on the note, or by making it darker or brighter, playing it with a slight hesitation, making it a bit longer or shorter (called *agogic*), giving it a more abrupt attack, changing the timbre, or doing any number of other things, depending on your taste, what you feel that note calls for.

Music also has accents not indicated by accent marks, going on all the time. There may be accents at the beginning of each bar, or implied accents on any note of the bar, depending on the grouping of the notes. Accents can occur through jumps in register or changes in orchestration. Accents occur through melodic and harmonic means, including using nonharmonic tones, anticipations, appoggiaturas, and grace notes. Any special articulation that brings notes out of the texture can be considered an accent. Accents help to make the rhythm "happen"; they're the spice in music.

Accents help to produce phrasing.

Phrasing

Phrasing is the way in which notes are organized for performance. The basic phrasing is indicated by the meter, the time signature, and the bar lines. Then, in addition, music is phrased through the use of accents, dynamics, melody and harmony, tone color, and other rhythmic play, often indicated by phrase markings (such as those used in example 1.19 to show the intended groupings of eighth notes). Phrasing is the way the notes are grouped and shaped. Musical expression is accomplished through phrasing.

Expression

Expression is the human element that goes beyond the notes on the page, the communication of feeling inside each individual performer. It is achieved through the use of phrasing along with rhythmic and melodic interpretation and control. In language, it would be the difference between a speech delivered by a computer, each word exactly the same, and a speech given by an orator, grouping words expressively, communicating feeling.

Two aspects of expressive techniques are rubato and nuance.

Rubato

Rubato is one kind of rhythmic manipulation of time. It comes from the Italian term *tempo rubato,* or stolen time. It strictly refers to slowing down some notes in a phrase, "robbing time" from them, and then giving the time back later in the phrase, to make up for the "crime." In the strict practice of rubato, one always wants to rob and then give back the same amount of time, so that the underlying pulse is not altered. In contemporary performance practice, rubato refers to almost any temporary speeding up and slowing down. It generally means to take the music "out of time" and play it freely, but just for a moment.

Nuance

Nuance is subtlety of expression, the means of expressing shades of personality and feeling. The ways in which to do it are as numerous as there are performers on the planet. Nuance often has to do with rhythmic shading, including rubato, placing notes a bit ahead of or behind the beat, the lengths of notes, accents and phrasing. Bending notes or playing slightly sharp or flat for expression is nuance. Dynamics also contribute to nuance, by building up to and dying away from certain notes, and by using all levels of volume. Tone color also plays a large part. Nuance is everything the musician does to make each note sound special.

BOOK

2

Improving Your Sense of Rhythm

Improving Your Sense of Rhythm

There are three realms to turn to for improving your rhythmic sense: the inner world of your own body and mind; the external world around you of sights, sounds, people, and teachers; and third, the realm of physical motion. This book's approach to improving sense of rhythm starts with resources in our hearts and minds, convenient and always available, including the inner world of imagination. Many find working with an external resource—a metronome, for example—to be the most tangible method, the one that seemingly leads most directly to "results." But all three areas lead to results; all contribute to the goal of strengthening pulse and improving rhythmic sense, and can be practiced concurrently.

If you work on these suggestions, your sense of rhythm will undoubtedly improve. With practice and attention, everyone's rhythm gets better.

IMPROVING PULSE AND RHYTHM USING INTERNAL SOURCES

Internal sources for improving rhythm include your imagination, inner pulse, breath, heartbeat, and muscles.

Imagination

Improving musical performance occurs in the imagination, and virtually all the suggestions in this book use imagination as part of the process. The first step is to imagine pulse.

Inner Pulse

Developing the inner pulse is essential for improving rhythm. Sense of pulse is what people usually mean by "sense of rhythm." Having a good sense of rhythm entails having the ability to produce a pulse inside oneself, without an external musical source and without relying on physical motion. The questions are, how do you do it, what does it feel like, and how do you improve it?

Before creating a pulse entirely in the imagination, create a pulse physically, an "outer" pulse. Tap your foot or hand, move your head, click your teeth or tongue, snap your fingers—whatever comes naturally to you. Produce a pulse for a while at whatever tempo feels right at the moment. Pay close attention to what you're doing; note what it sounds, feels, and looks like. Watch and listen to yourself. Memorize and internalize everything about the action.

Then stop what you are doing and imagine doing the same thing at the same tempo, as palpably as possible. Visualize it, and hear the sound in your mind. Got it? There it is, an inner pulse, in your imagination.

Try again with another action. Pick a musical motion, use it to keep a pulse for a while, internalize it, then stop moving and imagine it. There's another inner pulse. It's simple.

The more you imagine pulse, the stronger your sense of inner pulse will be. Imagine various motions, various feelings, at a wide variety of tempos. The more you develop it, the deeper you feel it, the more you can depend on it during performance.

I find the strongest place to imagine and feel the inner pulse is in the center of the chest, often considered the feeling center of the body. The more work you do there, the more tangibly you'll feel the pulse—*feel* not just in the physical sense but also in the emotional. The more you're connected with the pulse, the more of an emotional experience it becomes. Desire, musical expression, and pulse all get mixed together in the center of the chest.

Three basic means to develop the pulse in the chest are the breath, the heart, and the chest muscles.

Breath

The breath is convenient, powerful, and always with you, right in the center of the chest. You can control the rhythm of it.

Here are some suggestions for using your breath to improve your sense of rhythm:

1. Just sit and breathe. Let your breath occur at an even, comfortable rate that you can maintain for as long as you feel like. Feel your breath as a steady pulse. Imagine the words "in" while you breathe in and "out" while you breathe out.

2. Subdivide each breath. Maintaining the breathing groove, subdivide first in half, imagining the words "in and out and in and out and," with the "ands" occurring at the midpoint of each breath, like eighth notes. Then subdivide into 16ths, imagining "*in* e and a *out* e and a *in* e and a," subdividing each breath into groups of four. Then try "*in* trip let *out* trip let," subdividing each breath into triplets. Go on to

quintuplets ("*in* two three four five *out* two three four five,"), then sextuplets, and septuplets. Subdivide triplets into three beats each for nanuplets.

3. Mix up the subdivisions: subdivide the *in* breath into triplets and the *out* breath into 16ths, and repeat for a while. Create patterns, longer series of subdivisions—for example, try subdividing four breaths in and out in the following manner: in two, out three, in four, out five, in six, out five, in four, out three—and repeat the series over and over. Use your imagination to make up other patterns. Remember and return to patterns you like. Go to them during this practice, and let yourself sink into a long, deep, comfortable groove.

4. Maintain the breath groove, and imagine one of the actions mentioned above, the fingers snapping or the foot tapping, in conjunction with your breath and the subdivisions.

5. Count each breath, starting with "one," and count as high you can. This helps both the inner pulse and your ability to count bars, which is an important skill, especially for brass and percussion players. Counting to a hundred is good for building concentration.

6. Play around with the rhythm of the breath. Maintaining an even count, try breathing in for four, hold for two, out for four, hold for two (hear in your mind "in two three four—hold two—out two three four—hold two," each syllable getting one beat). This creates a pattern of 12 beats. Try a pattern of eight (in for three, hold one, out for three, and hold one). Feel the inner-pulse breath pattern; create your own.

If you feel yourself running out of breath, becoming a little uncomfortable, just let the tempo speed up or slow down.

The ends of one breath and the beginnings of another should be easy—no sharp edges, each breath rounded. Eliminate effort.

Incidentally, these breathing exercises are similar to many meditation techniques. That's good. Meditation can improve attention and concentration and help you stay both calm and alert. Meditation can help with your general well being, which can in turn benefit performance.

Working on your breath is a plus also because being aware of your breath can be useful during performance. If you find yourself nervous, chances are that you are breathing shallowly. By consciously slowing down the rhythm of your breath, you can often calm yourself. Conscious breathing can help you regain or maintain a strong inner pulse, stay calm, and return to your center. Your breath is your ally.

Heartbeat

While the heartbeat is not a very steady pulse musically speaking, your heart is still a valuable source of inner pulse.

Various ways to get in touch with your heartbeat include putting your hands on your chest or putting your fingers on the side of your neck. Probably the best way is to place two fingers on that spot so often used to feel pulse, on the underside of your wrist, on the thumb side, just about an inch away from where the hand starts.

Quietly spend some time feeling it as a musical pulse. What does it feel like? Is it strong? Does it speed up and slow down? Could you play music with it? Imagine a piece of music while feeling your pulse, using your heartbeat as the underlying pulse.

Organize your heartbeat into various meters. Imagine it in 2/4, 3/4, and so on. Subdivide it in various ways, as outlined in the breath exercises. Phrase your pulse.

Try organizing your heartbeat with your breath, and feel the rhythms that occur with the synchronization of your breath and heartbeat. Feel the pulse speed up with the *in* breath, and slow down with the *out* breath.

Feel the heart pulsing in the chest, and imagine it. When you can strongly imagine the feeling of the heart pulsing, you can access that imagined heartbeat to create a strong inner pulse. It becomes a tangible physical metaphor for pulse, which can be helpful, especially for slow tempos.

Chest Muscles

You can deepen and strengthen the feeling of pulse in the chest by exercising the chest and stomach muscles.

Put your hand on your solar plexus and push out, using the diaphragm muscles. Let's call this the chest pulse. While the center of feeling is in the chest, the stomach pushes out, because the ribs are in the way.

A sound can be associated with this action. Say "taah," and think and feel a lift. This gives the pulse life and energy. If you leave your mouth open, and continue to breathe, you hear a "hunh" kind of sound. You can also say "unhh" when you do it. The sound isn't necessary, but it can help.

Create a chest pulse this way, at whatever tempo feels appropriate at the moment. Feel your upper stomach pushing out into the hand, and hear the "taah" or "hunh" sound. Each breath is a little more energetic than usual, with emphasis on the front edge. What is important is the chest pulse, not the sound. You can get multiple pulses on each exhalation (12 is about my limit), and you can make the pulses and sounds on inhalations as well.

Some musicians make pulse sounds during performance. While the sounds can be exciting, and can help the group pulse together, it can also be distracting. Therefore, after getting used to the feeling and the sound, it is good to chest-pulse silently. When you get used to it, you can then disassociate it completely from the breath. Using the imagination, you can chest-pulse entirely in your mind as well.

Many find chest pulse the most powerful inner pulse. Use it to deepen and internalize the pulse of any music you are practicing or performing. Feeling the pulse in your chest for a bar or two before playing will always help performance.

More Imagination Techniques

Practice music entirely in the imagination, away from your instrument. Do it whenever you can, while walking, sitting, standing in a line, or riding in a train, plane, or car. It can help if you close your eyes. Think of the music, and imagine the pulse. Then imagine the music various ways, such as the following:

1. See the music on the page; watch and hear the notes go by in tempo.
2. Imagine your fingers on the instrument, and feel yourself performing.
3. Perform without touching the instrument, like a mime.
4. Imagine watching yourself playing, with a strong pulse. Do you like your performance?
5. Imagine the instrument playing itself, without you there. Hear it and feel it as tangibly as possible.
6. Imagine hearing the music as completely as possible, with pitch, harmony, phrasing, and all the colors.
7. Change the dynamics, phrasing, and balance in your mind. Hear the piece transposed to another instrument.

Do all these only as fast as you can clearly imagine them; don't rush it. If you're not clearly hearing or seeing all the notes, slow down. Hold the tempo. The slower it is, the better.

Imagining can often accomplish more than practicing your instrument. Also, your practice will be more solid and successful when you return to playing your instrument. This process can also help you learn pieces away from the instrument, which is useful.

At auditions, remember to do a bit of imagining before you dive into playing the excerpt. One bar of setting the tempo and imagining the music will help settle your performance.

The imagination is where the most progress can be made. Continue to strengthen and deepen your imagination in as many ways as you can imagine. The following are a few more imagination exercises to deepen the sense of pulse.

Just imagine a pulse. Then attach a sound to the pulse. Give the pulse a pitch. Change the pitch while maintaining the pulse. Keep the pitch, but change the sound of it: hear a piano play the pitch, then a guitar, then a trombone, then timpani. Hear an interval pulse. Create harmonies, maintaining the pulse. Change colors, orchestrations, dynamics; use your imagination to hear a pulse a million different ways.

Imagine a pulse as some physical action: a ball bouncing, birds' wings, a sphere or heart pulsing in and out, waves crashing on the beach, sheep jumping over a fence, a clock pendulum or a metronome going back and forth—whatever comes to mind. It's nice to do when you are going to sleep. In bed is also a good time to practice imagining your music.

IMPROVING PULSE AND RHYTHM USING EXTERNAL SOURCES

The Metronome

The metronome "keeps time"; it is the standard for dividing time into precise increments. It is indispensable both for musical study and as a universal reference for tempo. It has an important place in music history, and in history in general.

The concept for metronomes goes back to the creation of clocks. Both are timekeeping instruments. The famous inventor Galileo Galilei discovered the concept of timekeeping by using a pendulum back in 1582 or '83. The pendulum was successfully applied to clocks about a century later.

A series of inventors tried to use pendulums to make metronomes but encountered difficulty in keeping the pendulum moving quickly, and in maintaining different tempos. Finally, in 1812, inventor Dietrik Winkel thought of putting two counterweights on the pendulum. This stroke of genius allowed a short pendulum to go both slowly and quickly, and made it easy to adjust its tempo.

Johann Maelzel, an inventor with a musical background, met and developed a relationship with Beethoven, and made some ear trumpets to help Beethoven hear. He also convinced Beethoven to write a piece that Maelzel later claimed as his own, and Beethoven apparently sued. Maelzel also claimed Winkel's metronomic idea as his own and in 1816 started manufacturing Maelzel's Metronome. This metronome has become the standard.

By moving one of the weights, you can control the speed of the pendulum. The pendulum has numbers on it, corresponding to the changing position of the weight on the pendulum. These marks show where to move the weight to produce the correct tempo, indicated by the tempo mark, written in music notation as "mm=," meaning "metronome mark equals." (Originally, "mm=" may have stood for Maelzel's Metronome.) This mark indicates the frequency of clicks per minute produced by the metronome. That is, the number 40 on the metronome pendulum indicates that there are 40 clicks per minute, the 200 mark indicates 200 clicks per minute, and so on.

These days metronomes come in various shapes and forms—mechanical, electrical, and digital, including a circular design I'm developing. The metronome-mark tempo on the modern models is indicated on a display, as there is no pendulum rocking back and forth. But the clicks per minute, the mm=, remain standard.

The metronome can be your best friend in your quest for rhythmic excellence. Find one you like, easy to use, with a pleasing sound.

The following exercises suggest ways to use the metronome for the development of inner pulse, and for improvement of musical performance in general.

Metronome Exercises Part 1 outlines a course of study using only the metronome, away from your major instruments, focusing strictly on your inner timekeeper. Part 2 suggests ways to use the metronome while practicing with your instrument.

Everyone is at a different level of familiarity with the metronome. Find the sections that feel right for you. Even if you are an experienced metronome user, it is worthwhile to review the basics, getting ever deeper into the pulse.

The point of these exercises is not to "finish" them, to do once and move on. Working on pulse is a lifelong process. Use these exercises as starting points, work on sections that feel right, move around, from easy to hard and back again. It's good to work on your inner pulse first thing every day.

Work on these as long as feels comfortable. If you are at a stage in which you want to make leaps and bounds of rhythmic improvement, work on this 40 minutes to an hour a day. If you are on a "rhythmic maintenance" schedule, work much less on them, five to 15 minutes a day. The amount of time spent is determined by your motivation, and where you're at in your career. Whatever routine you are in, concentrate, and sink deeply into the pulse. If your mind wanders, either regain focus or stop. As in all practice, better five minutes of focused attention than an hour of listless drifting.

I've used the standard "mm=", to indicate tempos. They are just suggestions. Once you feel more or less comfortable in one tempo, go faster or slower, especially slower. Try many tempos, challenge yourself, and keep track of your progress.

Metronome Exercises Part 1: Working on Pulse Away from Your Main Instrument

You need a staccato percussion instrument for these exercises. Claves, the two short and thick wooden sticks used in Latin music, are best. Clapping your hands also works, as does hitting a stick against a desk.

Sit in a position that you can hold comfortably for an extended period of time, so that you can sink into the pulse. Have the metronome within easy reach.

Metronome Exercise 1: Imagining the Metronome

Set the metronome at a moderate tempo, around mm=80. Just listen to the sound of the metronome. Memorize and internalize the sound. Turn off the metronome and imagine the sound you were hearing. Listen to the metronome in your head.

Turn the metronome back on, and check yourself. Make sure you are hearing that sound, and at that exact tempo. Try it a few times, until you can tangibly imagine the metronome. Change the tempo, and do it again.

Metronome Exercise 2: Imagining Your Sound

With the metronome turned off, take the claves and just play them for a while, memorizing the sound. Spend a while getting used to the instrument.

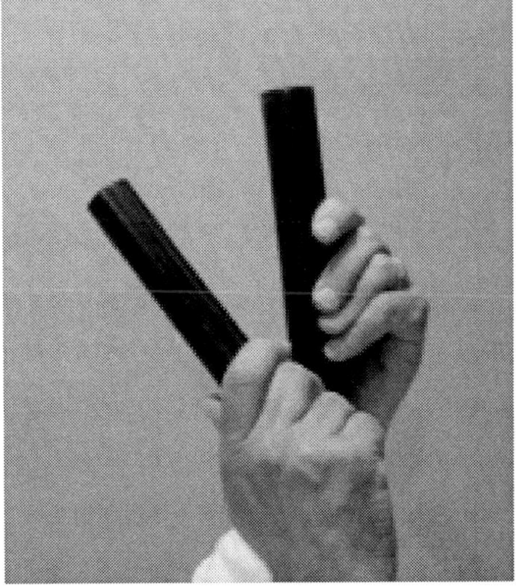

Hold one clave firmly but without tension in one hand, as shown on left. Form a resonant chamber with the palm of the same hand, as shown on right.

Strike one clave with the other, right above the resonant chamber. Play a bit. Memorize the sound. Stop playing and imagine the sound.

Do Metronome Exercise 1 again, this time tangibly imagining the clave sound instead of the metronome sound.

Metronome Exercise 3: Imagining Then Playing with the Metronome

Now play the clave pulse you were imagining, still with the metronome off. Play it for a little while. Stop and imagine it. Then play it again. Alternate back and forth between imagining and playing the pulse. When you play it, concentrate on making your performance as steady as the pulse sound you are imagining.

Check back with the metronome, turn it on and see if you are still at 80. Turn off the metronome, imagine the pulse again, and then see how long you can play the pulse steadily. Try it at mm=60, 100, 140, and 40. Alternate between listening to the metronome, turning it off, imagining the pulse, and playing the pulse. Stop whenever you have had enough.

Once your pulse feels pretty steady, move on to playing the pulse while the metronome is on.

When playing along with the metronome, the sound of the claves should be as close to the metronome as possible—so close, in fact, that you don't actually hear the metronome. You want the sound of the claves to cover, or hide, the metronome. This is called hiding or burying the metronome.

If you don't completely hide the metronome with your clave sound, a *flam*—two percussive sounds in very close proximity—will be produced. A flam indicates that you are not exactly in time with the metronome.

The goal is to avoid flams. Remember, though, that hiding the metronome is not easy to do. Don't get frustrated. No one hides the metronome all the time. Just keep working on getting the notes closer together.

The reason these exercises should be done with a very short percussive sound is that longer sounds can carry over and hide the metronome even when you play slightly ahead, which can train you to play ahead of the beat. Be careful of that. That's why a pair of crisp claves works better than a drum or a cowbell.

Metronome Exercises 4 through 9 delve into hiding the metronome. The sound of the metronome is represented by notes below the line, and the notes to be played are written above the line.

Metronome Exercise 4: Fours

Set the metronome to a moderate tempo, mm=80 to 96. Turn it on and leave it on. Alternate between listening to the metronome for four beats and playing with the metronome for four beats, as follows:

EXAMPLE 2.1

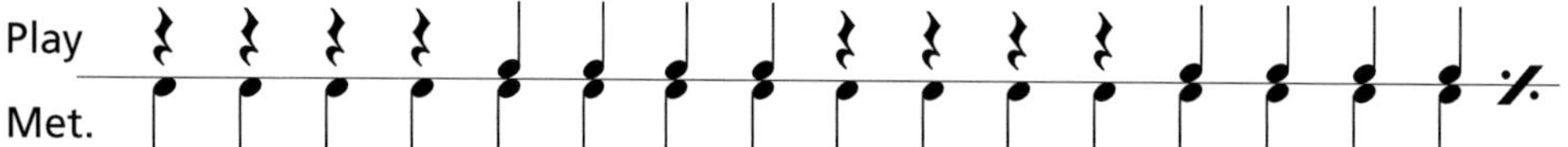

Listen for four beats, play four, listen four, play four, back and forth, on and on, until you feel that the four notes you play sound just like the four notes you are listening to. Take your time and sink into it.

Metronome Exercise 5: Threes

This is the same as the last exercise, but in a pattern of threes, as follows:

EXAMPLE 2.2

Listen to three, play three, listen, play, back and forth, sinking ever deeper.

Metronome Exercise 6: Twos

This time use a pattern of twos:

EXAMPLE 2.3

Make sure your two played beats sound rhythmically exactly like the metronome, and that you do not hear the metronome during the beats that you play. Eliminate flams.

Metronome Exercise 7: Ones, or Alternation

Play one beat, listen to one beat, play one, listen to one, back and forth.

EXAMPLE 2.4

This one is great for sinking deeply into the pulse. Feel the rhythm created by the alternation. Keep hiding the metronome.

Metronome Exercise 8: Longer Phrases and Varied Groupings

Play the patterns outlined in the preceding four exercises, but with longer phrases. Try alternating between playing and listening for five beats, six beats, seven beats, and eight beats.

Use your imagination to vary the patterns, alternating ones for a while, then twos, then fours, then fives or more. Improvise.

One nice pattern is to play one, rest one, play two, rest one, play three, rest one, play four, rest one, play five, rest one, going ever higher, as long as you can hide the metronome. With longer phrases, you'll want to listen less and play more, because it gets boring to listen to 10 metronome beats in a row. Keep hiding the metronome. Be creative; play around with ideas. The following is one suggestion:

EXAMPLE 2.5

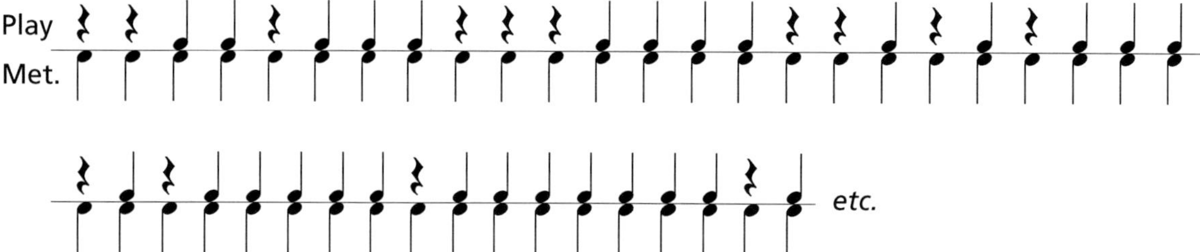

Challenge yourself every day. Try faster tempos and, more importantly, try slower ones—the slower the better. Try a little slower every day, and keep track of your progress.

Metronome Exercise 9: The Pulse Unison

The pulse unison is just like the pitch unison; it means play the same pulse at the same time. Turn on the metronome, listen for a bit, and then play along. See how long you can play a pulse unison. Count how many beats fall exactly together without a flam. The longer you can go without hearing one, the better. Keep track of your progress. If you can count up to 20 without a flam, try it a little slower. If you really sink into the groove you'll wonder if the metronome broke.

EXAMPLE 2.6

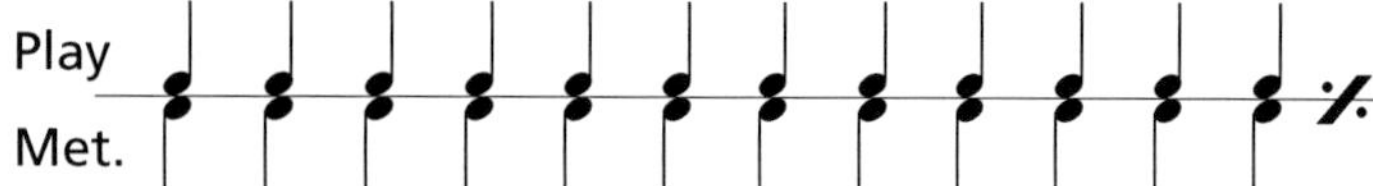

Metronome Exercise 10: The Displaced Pulse Unison

To play a displaced pulse unison means to play the same pulse as the metronome, but place your beats so that they do not sound with the metronome. You can have an almost infinite variety of displaced pulse unisons. We will look at pulse unisons displaced by eighths, 16ths, and triplets.

Start by playing a pulse at exactly the halfway point between the metronome pulses, the eighth-note subdivision.

Set the metronome to mm=60. Turn it on and leave it on. First imagine the "ands" of each metronome pulse. Then perform the following:

EXAMPLE 2.7

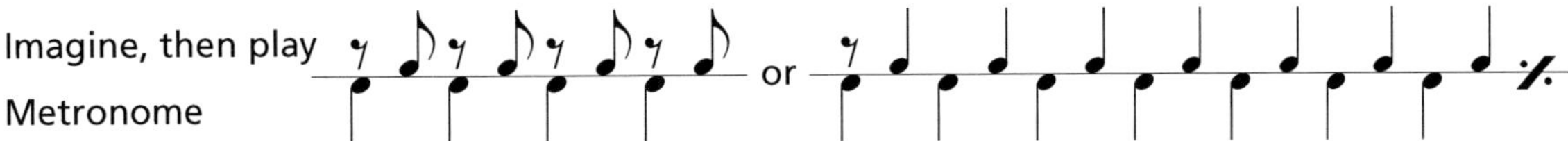

There are two ways to feel this. One way is to feel yourself playing the "ands" to the metronome quarter notes, feeling each eighth subdivision, dividing each pulse into two. The other way is to feel that you are playing the same pulse as the metronome, just displaced exactly in between each beat. Let go of the subdivisions, and it becomes one smooth pulse flow.

Stop playing for a moment and imagine the combined pulse of the metronome and the "ands" as just one pulse. The combined pulse tempo of both the metronome pulse and your pulse is mm=120—twice as fast as the metronome pulse.

Play again and let go of subdividing the metronome pulse. See if you can feel the pulse you play as one smooth pulse occurring concurrently with the smooth metronome pulse, creating one smooth, combined pulse twice as fast as the metronome by itself.

This exercise is excellent for sinking into a strong groove. Keep at it until you feel one calm, steady pulse created by both you and the metronome.

This exercise is also a good indication of your level of relaxation. As you move the metronome up to faster tempos, you will find that you cannot perform this exercise unless you can remain quite relaxed. Keep moving the metronome up to faster tempos and monitor how fast you can go and the level of relaxation necessary to do so. Work on this, and be able to perform it at mm=206 without a hitch. If you can perform it at mm=240, you really have it.

You can displace a pulse unison anywhere within the beat.

Set the metronome to mm=60 again, and leave it on. Imagine the metronome pulse divided into 16ths. Count "e + a" for each 16th, then imagine them between every metronome pulse, really hearing them in your mind.

EXAMPLE 2.8

Next, play the following, first by subdividing each pulse, and then by performing an even pulse that is displaced one 16th after each metronome pulse.

EXAMPLE 2.9

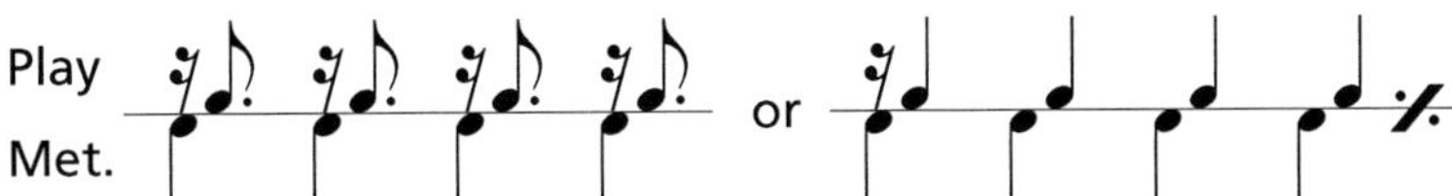

Feel and hear the rhythm created by your playing and the metronome as one rhythm.

Next, perform the following in the same manner:

EXAMPLE 2.10

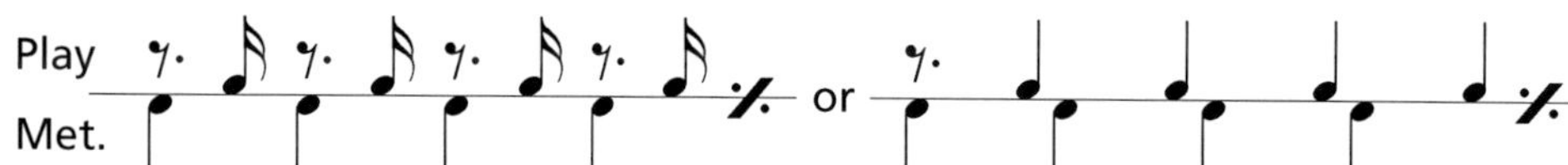

Again, once you have it, see if you can let go of subdividing, and perform as if it is a "pulse duet" with the metronome—one pulse, two sounds.

Now let's move to triplets. First, just listen to the metronome at mm=60, and imagine the triplets.

EXAMPLE 2.11

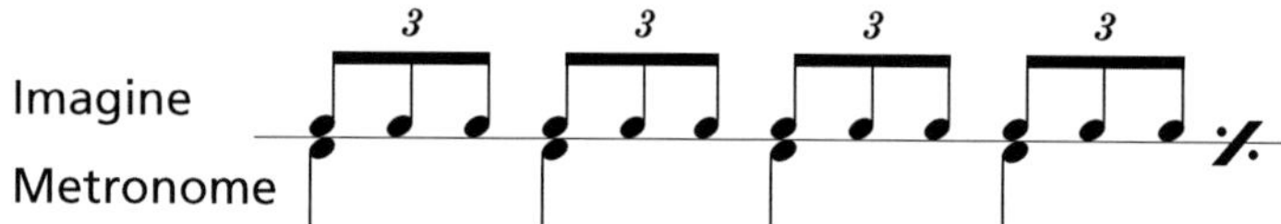

Now perform the second triplet of the metronome pulse, as follows:

EXAMPLE 2.12

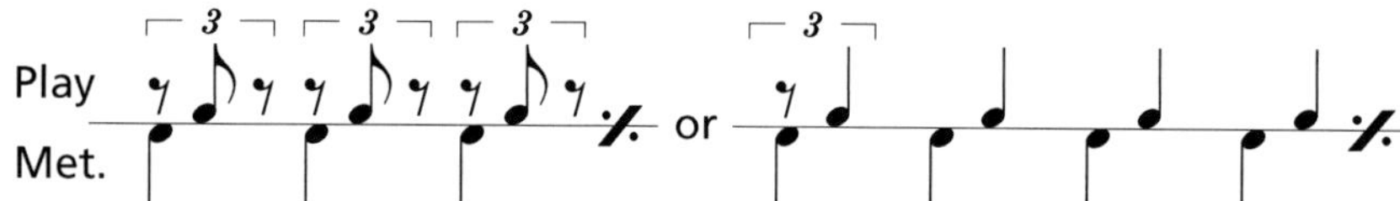

Then perform the third triplet of each metronome pulse, as follows:

EXAMPLE 2.13

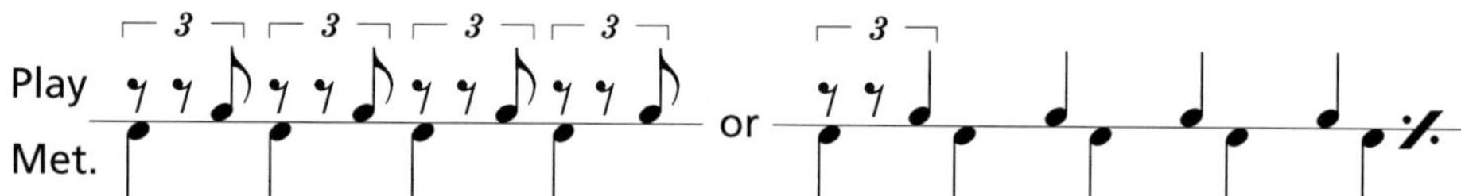

Feel these exercises three different ways:

1. You are subdividing each beat of the metronome into triplets.
2. You are playing a smooth pulse displaced by triplets.
3. You feel the combined rhythm of your playing and the metronome.

The combined rhythm of your playing a displaced pulse in triplets in combination with the metronome results in the following two rhythms:

EXAMPLE 2.14

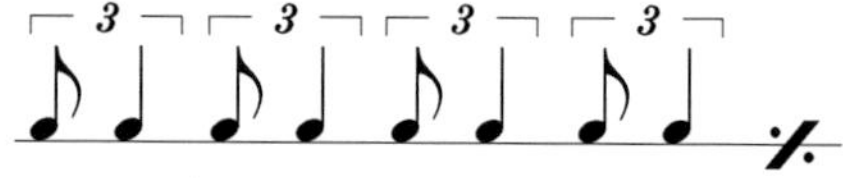

and

EXAMPLE 2.15

Sink into these, feel them in all three ways. Challenge yourself with slower and faster tempos, and stay relaxed, as tension hinders progress.

The following exercises go further with subdivisions. When subdividing the pulse, feel a chest pulse on the main beats. That, as outlined on page 2▪5, is accomplished with an exertion, real or imagined, in the center of your chest. This will help internalize and deepen the pulse.

Metronome Exercise 11: Eighths

Set the metronome at mm=80. Listen and imagine eighths. Then imagine and play the following two rhythms:

EXAMPLE 2.16

EXAMPLE 2.17

Then alternate back and forth between the two:

EXAMPLE 2.18

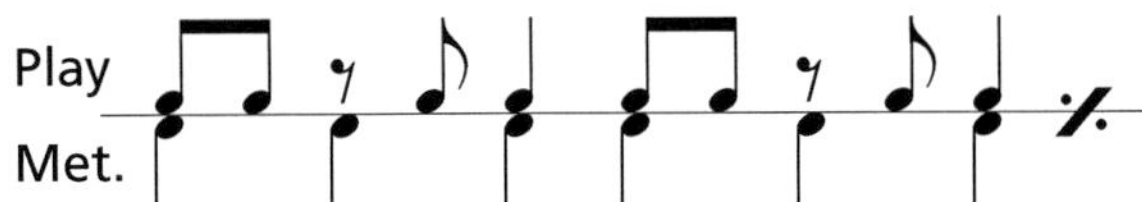

Play an even pulse of eighths, hiding the metronome well:

EXAMPLE 2.19

The pulse you are playing is twice as fast as the metronome, also known as one octave above the metronome. Stop now and then to check in with the metronome, then sink into a smooth, even groove for a while.

Make up exercises and improvise using eighths. Here is a short suggestion:

EXAMPLE 2.20

Metronome Exercise 12: Triplets

Set the metronome to mm=60 and leave it on. Imagine the triplet subdivisions of each pulse. Then perform the following two figures:

EXAMPLE 2.21

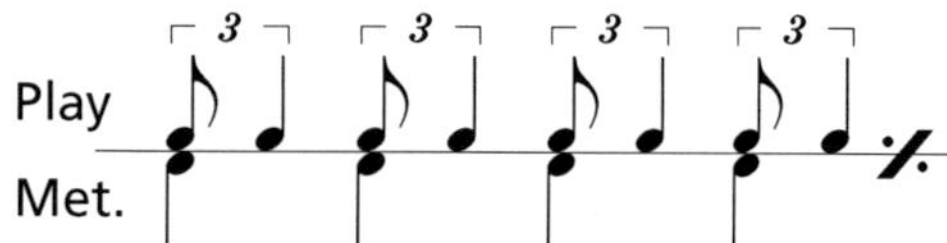

EXAMPLE 2.22

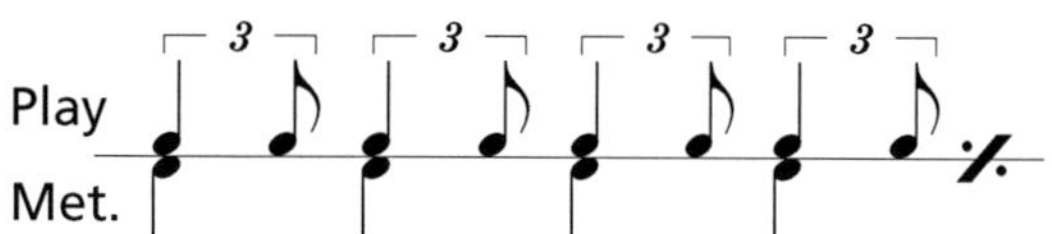

Work on exercises 2.12 and 2.13 again, and then play around with the triplets. Make up patterns. Alternate bars of silence with triplet patterns. Imagine triplets in the rests while you play patterns and improvise. Here is a triplet study:

EXAMPLE 2.23

Metronome Exercise 13: 16ths

Keeping the metronome set to mm=60, imagine 16ths, imagine the following patterns, and perform:

EXAMPLE 2.24

EXAMPLE 2.25

EXAMPLE 2.26

The following pattern can be accomplished by subdividing each beat and playing the two appropriate 16ths, or by feeling the pulse at mm =120, an octave above the metronome pulse, and displaced one 16th. This way of looking at it helps avoid "stabbing" at the notes, and helps to sink into a calm, smooth groove.

EXAMPLE 2.27

The next one is all the 16ths, a frequency two octaves above the metronome pulse. Relax and hide the metronome. Stop and check in every once in a while, imagining the 16ths.

EXAMPLE 2.28

Improvise and imagine every 16th in the silences you don't play. You can also perform smoothly without imagining every silent 16th. Chest-pulse on the beats. Take time to also concentrate on your breathing, calming it down, settling the pulse. Perform as if the metronome is another player; play a duet with it. Here is a short suggestion, then make up your own:

EXAMPLE 2.29

Metronome Exercise 14: Advanced Subdivisions—Quintuplets and Beyond

Go through the routines outlined in the previous metronome exercises using quintuplets, sextuplets, septuplets, and 32nd notes. Start by imagining, then play. Here is a quintuplet study. Set the metronome to mm=44.

EXAMPLE 2.30

Slow the metronome down for smaller subdivisions. Try mm=44 for sextuplets and mm=30 for septuplets and 32nd notes, if your metronome goes down there. Imagine, sink in, and hide the metronome. It's not necessary to provide written combinations for sextuplets, septuplets, and 32nd notes; you can come up with your own based on the exercises provided so far. I do, however, want to touch on the nines.

Metronome Exercise 15: Nanuplets

Nines are usually played by subdividing triplets by triplets.

Set the metronome to 30, or as slow as possible. Listen to the metronome, and imagine triplets.

EXAMPLE 2.31

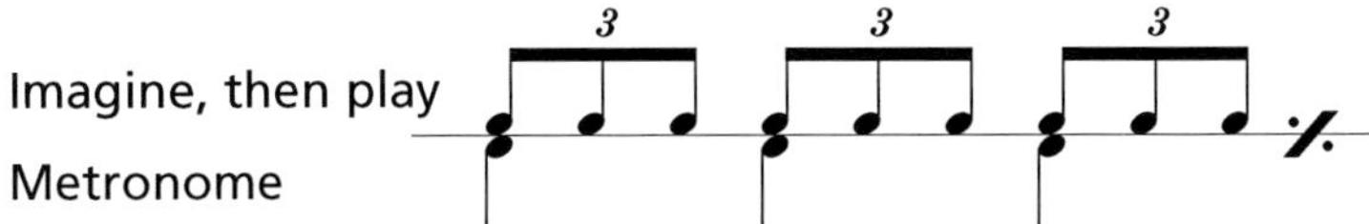

Imagine subdividing the triplets with triplets.

EXAMPLE 2.32

There are the nines. Next, while imagining this pattern, play the bigger triplets from example 2.31. Then play all nine. Don't push the tempo:

Here's a triplet nines exercise:

EXAMPLE 2.33

Now let go of the triplets, and play nines as nines, without the triplet subdivision. Keeping the metronome at 30, imagine nines phrased without triplets, as suggested below. Once you can hear them in the imagination, perform them.

EXAMPLE 2.34

Practicing fives, sevens, and especially nines helps you phrase freely within a strong pulse.

The next set of metronome exercises, 16 through 20, involve switching between the above subdivisions.

Metronome Exercise 16: Eighths and 16ths

Set the metronome to 52. Imagine and perform the following:

EXAMPLE 2.35

EXAMPLE 2.36

EXAMPLE 2.37

Spend time improvising with both eighths and 16ths.

Metronome Exercise 17: Eighths and Triplets

Keep the metronome at 52, and imagine the following until it feels clear and solid:

EXAMPLE 2.38

This is the hemiola, the fundamental polyrhythm. Imagine it, and then play it in a relaxed and strong manner. Get it right, make it easy. This one's important.

Imagine and practice the following rhythms. Don't rush the eighths, drag the triplets, or vice versa.

EXAMPLE 2.39

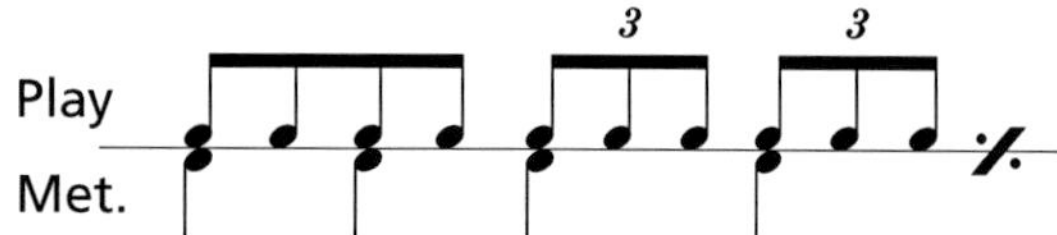

Feel the difference between the eighth and triplet rests:

EXAMPLE 2.40

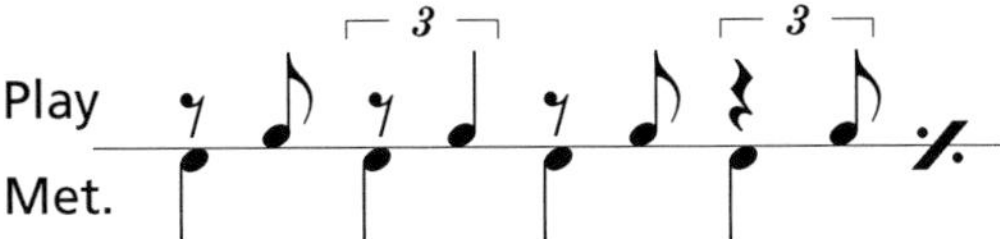

EXAMPLE 2.41

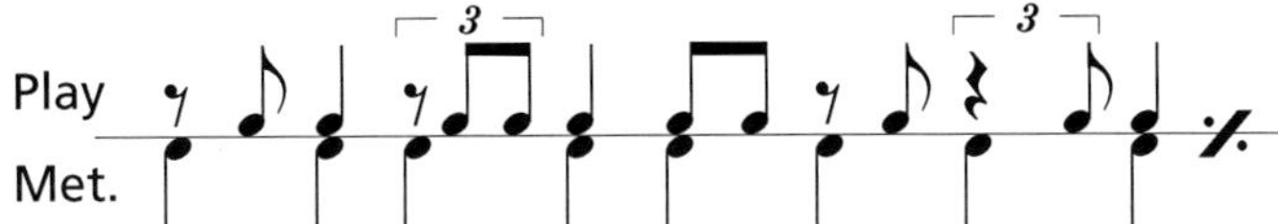

EXAMPLE 2.42

Make up your own. Try slower and faster tempos. Take your time, make it strong, feel comfortable, "fat"—that is, not pushing or pulling to get to the metronome in time. Settle the relationship between eighths and triplets.

Metronome Exercise 18: Triplets and 16ths

Keeping triplets and 16ths "fat" can be elusive rhythmically. Set the metronome to 48–52, and just imagine the following:

EXAMPLE 2.43

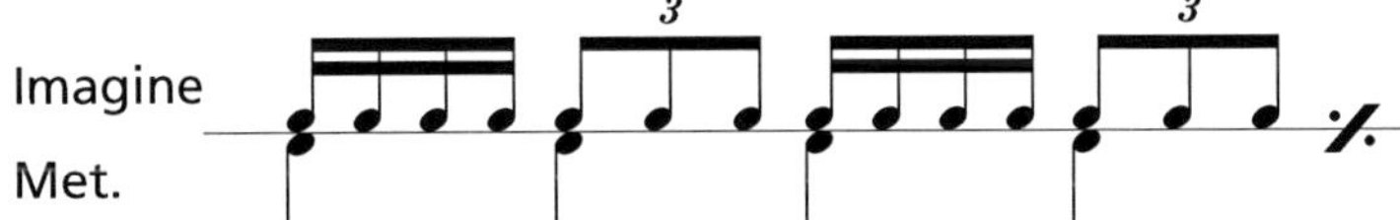

Sink in, feel it, and perform it fatly—no hurrying or slowing down, everything even.

Do the same routine with the following:

EXAMPLE 2.44

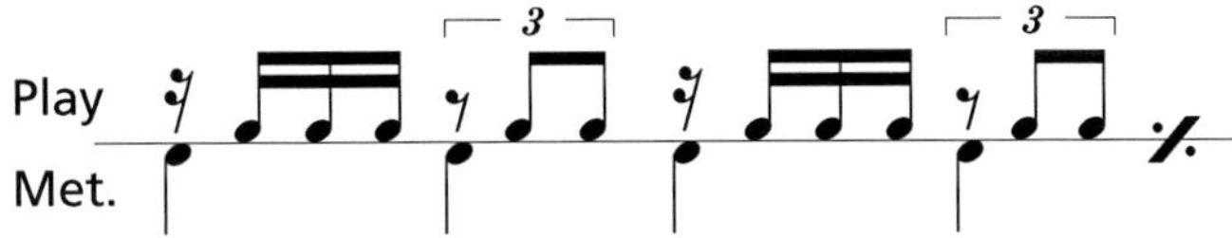

EXAMPLE 2.45

EXAMPLE 2.46

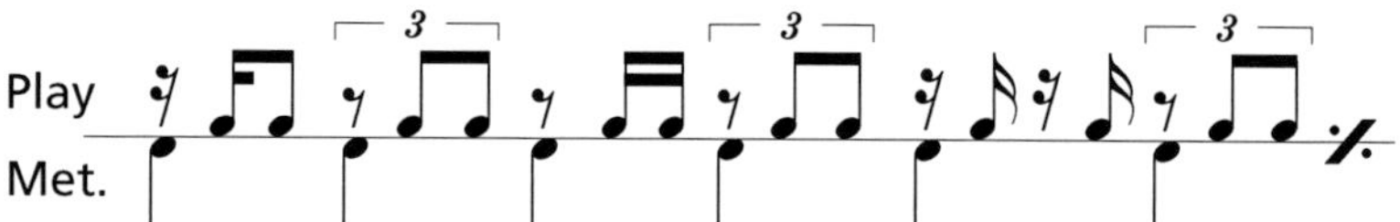

EXAMPLE 2.47

EXAMPLE 2.48

Improvise along these lines.

Metronome Exercise 19: Eighths, Triplets, and 16ths

Imagine the following for a while:

EXAMPLE 2.49

Perform it, first leaving out the metronome beats, listening to the metronome in the rests, as follows:

EXAMPLE 2.50

Then perform it fatly, hiding the metronome:

EXAMPLE 2.51

Improvise along these lines. Just make up whatever rhythm comes to you. The following exercises can help give you ideas. Avoid hurrying to get to the metronome on time.

EXAMPLE 2.52

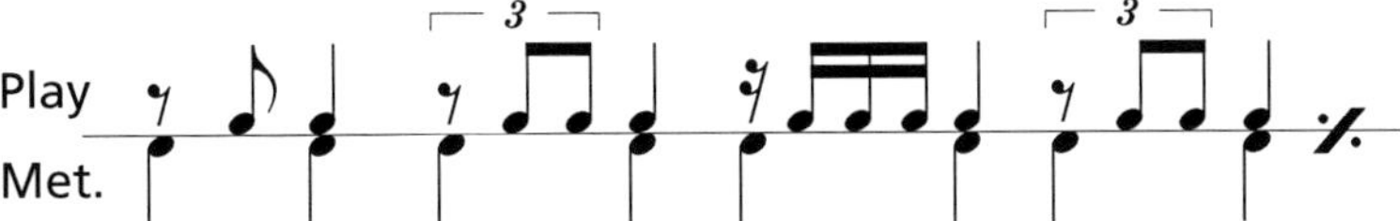

EXAMPLE 2.53

EXAMPLE 2.54

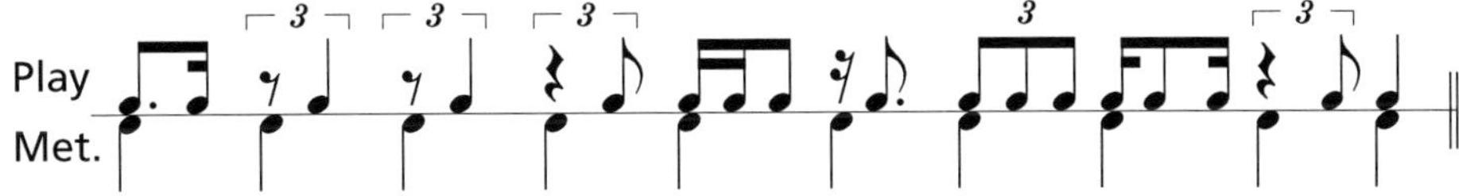

EXAMPLE 2.55

Notice your tendencies and correct them. Do you tend to rush the 16ths? Are you hurrying or slowing down at the end of a triplet figure to come to the metronome on time? Take your time, get it right.

Metronome Exercise 20: Eighths, Triplets, 16ths, Quintuplets, and Sextuplets

The following exercises incorporate quintuplets and sextuplets. Play them, and then make up your own.

EXAMPLE 2.56

EXAMPLE 2.57

EXAMPLE 2.58

EXAMPLE 2.59

EXAMPLE 2.60

EXAMPLE 2.61

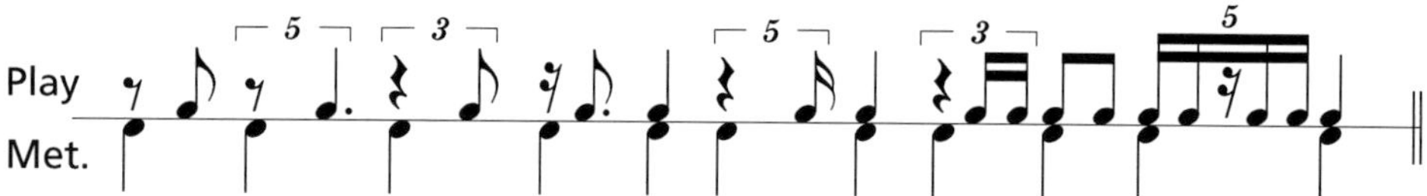

Metronome Exercise 21: Eighths, Triplets, 16ths, Quintuplets, Sextuplets, Septuplets, 32nds, and Nanuplets

It is better to practice just one pattern well than many more-or-less well. Keep your standards high. Practice just one, and do it well.

EXAMPLE 2.62

Metronome exercises 22 to 25 entail imagining the metronome as other than the main beat—that is, displacing it. These exercises strengthen the rhythmic imagination and facilitate freedom, phrasing, and flexibility. There are three steps to each exercise: (1) imagine, (2) count, and (3) play.

Metronome Exercise 22: Displacing the Metronome by Eighths

Set the metronome to 60. Hear it, imagine it, as follows:

EXAMPLE 2.63

Metronome

It may help to imagine it in 4/4, imagining or saying the count, as follows:

EXAMPLE 2.64

Count and play one (+) two (+) three (+) four (+)

Metronome

(and) (and) (and) (and)

Say the "ands" out loud at first, and then just imagine them.

Hear it phrased in three also, as follows:

EXAMPLE 2.65

Count and play one (+) two (+) three (+) one (+) two (+) three (+)

Metronome

(and) (and) (and) (and) (and) (and)

After you imagine and count, play and practice them with the metronome.

Metronome Exercise 23: Displacing the Metronome by 16ths

Continue this process, now imagining the metronome pulse displaced by 16ths. In 4/4, imagine the metronome as the "e" of each beat as follows:

EXAMPLE 2.66

Count and play 1 (e) + a 2 (e) + a 3 (e) + a 4 (e) + a

Metronome

(e) (e) (e) (e)

Count as long as you need to, and then let go of the count and just imagine the metronome as the "e" of every beat. Then perform the 16ths that you were counting, with the metronome.

Phrase it in three:

EXAMPLE 2.67

Count and play 1 (e) + a 2 (e) + a 3 (e) + a

Metronome

(e) (e) (e)

Now imagine the metronome as the "a":

EXAMPLE 2.68

Count and play 1 e + (a) 2 e + (a) 3 e + (a) 4 e + (a)
Metronome
(a) (a) (a) (a)

Count, then let go of the count and just feel it. Try performing the 1, e, and +, listening to the metronome play the a.

Also, let go of feeling it necessarily in three or four, and feel the metronome as an infinite displaced pulse.

Metronome Exercise 24: Displacing the Metronome by Triplets

Count, and then imagine, the following:

EXAMPLE 2.69

Count and play 1 (trip) let 2 (trip) let 3 (trip) let
Metronome
3 3 3
(trip) (trip) (trip)

EXAMPLE 2.70

Count and play 1 trip (let) 2 trip (let) 3 trip (let)
Metronome
3 3 3
(let) (let) (let)

When imagining the above, it helps to feel a chest pulse on the main beats, to disassociate the main beat from the metronome sound.

Metronome Exercise 25: Displaced Metronome Pulse Continued

Take Metronome Exercise 9, the pulse unison, and displace it all the ways outlined in exercises 22 through 24.

EXAMPLE 2.71

Play
Met.

EXAMPLE 2.72

Play
Met.

EXAMPLE 2.73

Play
Met.

EXAMPLE 2.74

EXAMPLE 2.75

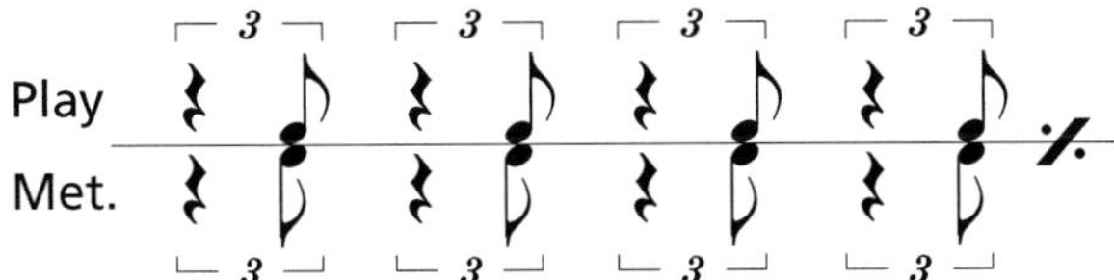

EXAMPLE 2.76

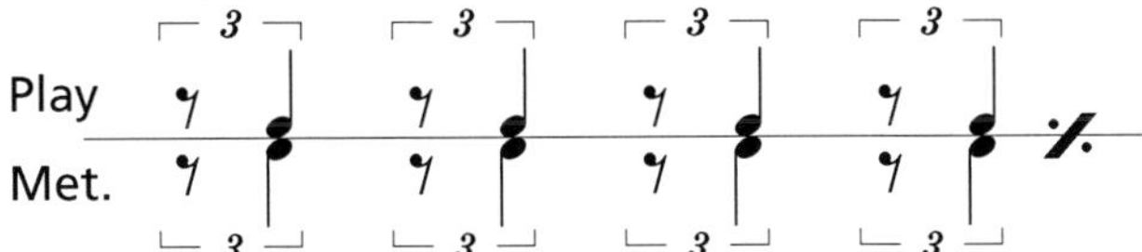

Go on to the displaced pulse unison introduced in Metronome Exercise 10. Play the main beats, imagining the metronome displaced all the ways outlined, with the metronome sounding off the beat. This takes some getting used to.

EXAMPLE 2.77

EXAMPLE 2.78

EXAMPLE 2.79

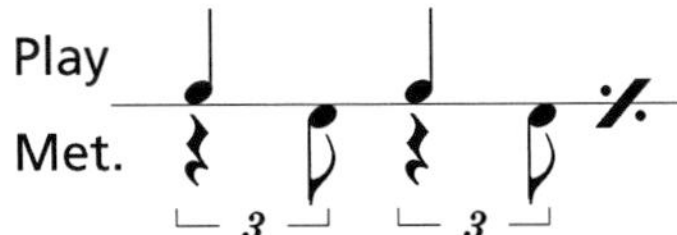

I think you get the idea. Feel the pulse in the chest, as you play and hear the metronome off the beat.

Go through Metronome Exercises 11 through 21, imagining the metronome displaced by eighths, 16ths, and triplets. Many will come easy, but others will entail some hard work, especially those involving quintuplets, septuplets, and nanuplets.

Use your imagination to displace the metronome in a logical way for each exercise.

Besides working on the written exercises, improvise over a metronome pulse, displaced in all the ways outlined. Let the written exercises be starting points.

For yet further practice, displace the metronome in a way that does not correspond to the exercise. By that I mean displace the metronome by triplets when studying eighth-note exercises, or by 16ths when studying triplet exercises. This isn't easy, keeping two separate subdivisions going in the mind at the same time, but it's a necessary strength for conductors and performers of contemporary music and a worthwhile pursuit for all contemporary musicians.

Metronome Exercise 26: Metronome Phrasing

Set the metronome to a fast click, 240 or faster, and listen to it. Phrase the metronome in your imagination the following ways:

EXAMPLE 2.80

EXAMPLE 2.81

EXAMPLE 2.82

EXAMPLE 2.83

Imagine these phrasings until you can internally phrase the metronome beats any which way.

Slow down the metronome, say to mm=180, and perform pulse unison in all the phrases outlined above. For example:

EXAMPLE 2.84

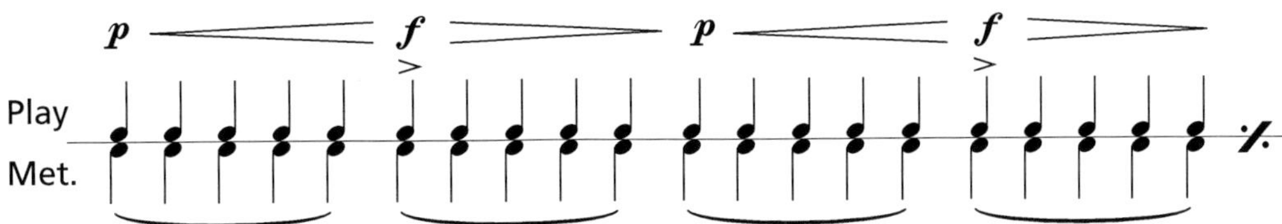

Phrase a pulse without speeding up or slowing down, without "coming apart" from the metronome. You can keep checking in with the metronome by putting rests into the exercise, and listening to the metronome for a phrase or two. As you get better you will be able to go for longer periods without stopping.

Crescendo toward and diminuendo away from the phrase markings, and also use sudden dynamics for the accents.

This exercise is important because it helps overcome the natural tendency to rush as you crescendo and drag as you diminuendo. Become sensitive to this common phenomenon.

Now perform all these phrasings while playing an evenly displaced pulse unison in threes. For example:

EXAMPLE 2.85

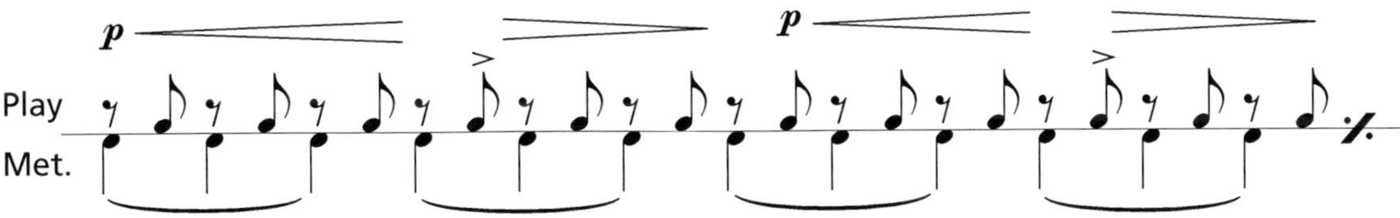

Phrase a displaced pulse unison in twos, threes, fours, fives, sixes, sevens, and combinations. You don't need them written out here. Start at mm=96, and practice until you can perform them at mm=160 to 180. These exercises are excellent for fluidity and strengthening the imagination. Continue to phrase using both sudden accents and dynamics.

Metronome Exercise 27: "Real" Rhythms

This exercise is every rhythm in music. Extract rhythms from the music you are practicing, and practice them as abstract metronome exercises, focusing entirely on pulse, rhythmic phrasing, and clarity. Hide the metronome when playing rhythms from your repertoire. Slow down problem rhythms, and get them right, lining up exactly to the pulse. Try displacing the pulse.

The following are a few examples of famous rhythms from famous pieces. Note the options of metronome placement in some of the following exercises:

EXAMPLE 2.86 Opening viola part from Johann Strauss's *Don Juan:*

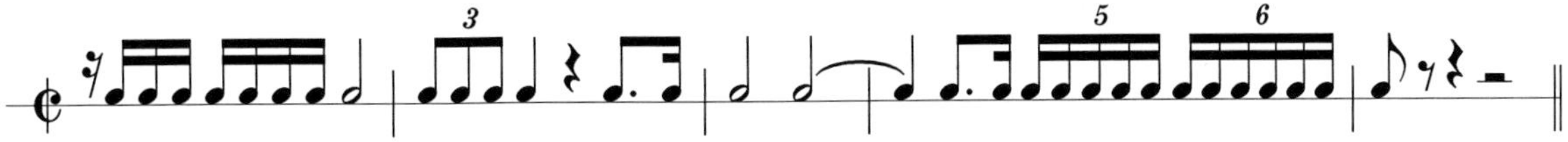

EXAMPLE 2.87 From the scherzo in Mendelssohn's *Midsummer Night's Dream:*

EXAMPLE 2.88 From opening of Strauss's *Death and Transfiguration:*

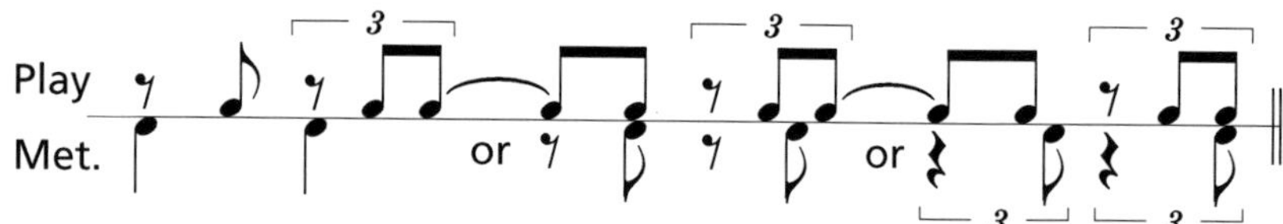

EXAMPLE 2.89 Lick for brass and timpani from Hindemith's *Symphonic Metamorphosis:*

EXAMPLE 2.90 Two bars of violin from Bartók's *Music for Strings, Percussion, and Celeste:*

EXAMPLE 2.91 Viola part from Dvorak's *New World Symphony:*

Studying your music in a purely rhythmic, abstract way will make your performance stronger.

That wraps up the abstract metronome exercises. Now we enter the realm of using the metronome while practicing with your instrument.

Metronome Exercises Part 2: Using the Metronome in Practice with Your Main Instrument

This section looks at some of the many ways a metronome can be used in daily instrument practice.

One important point: Don't let the metronome become a crutch. Spend as much time practicing without a metronome as with one. Bad habits result from relying on the metronome too much. You must ultimately rely on your inner pulse, not the metronome. To avoid this, practice also using the chest pulse instead of the metronome.

The ideas outlined in this section can apply to any excerpt. We will use a famous example, the opening theme for cello and viola in A♭ major, from the second movement of Beethoven's Fifth Symphony:

EXAMPLE 2.92

Metronome and Instrument Exercise 1

If you don't play cello or viola, transpose the excerpt to your instrument, play it on piano, or sing it with solfege.

The first instinct, and it is a good one, is to practice with the metronome marking every note that gets the beat, as indicated by the lower number in the time signature—in this case every eighth note, as follows.

Either use the indicated tempo, or pick a slower one. Slow practice often leads to quicker results. Also, it's wise to practice at various tempos, as you don't know what tempo the conductor or audition committee will ask for. We are going to use mm=90, as it is easily divisible by three.

EXAMPLE 2.93

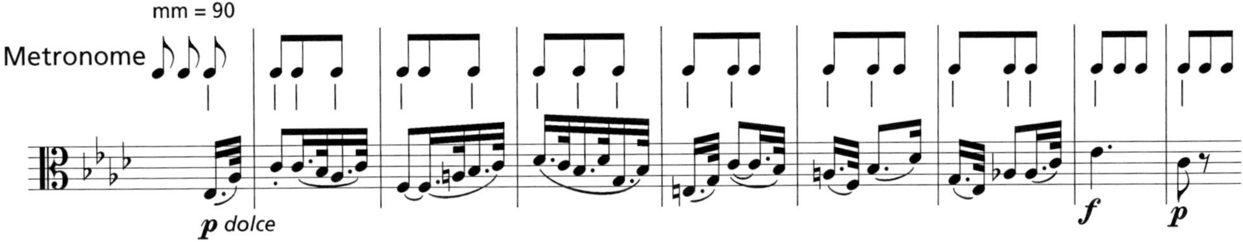

First, just imagine the excerpt while listening to the metronome at mm=90. Once you can hear it in your mind, practice, carefully lining up your notes with the metronome sound. The lines descending from the metronome pulse indicate where the music and the metronome sound exactly together.

Metronome and Instrument Exercise 2

The next step is to set the metronome to the bar line, the downbeat, the upper figure in the time signature. In this example, that process results in the metronome to be set at mm=30, as follows:

EXAMPLE 2.94

It is good to get intimate with this slow pulse to play this excerpt, to feel the phrase. Just listen to the metronome, and imagine the excerpt a few ways:

1. Hear it.
2. See the notes going by.
3. Imagine watching yourself play it.
4. Imagine yourself playing it, feeling the instrument in your imagination.

Imagine while listening to the metronome, and then without listening to the metronome, feeling the pulse in the chest.

Then play it, lining up every downbeat perfectly with the metronome. Feel the bar lines in your chest.

Metronome and Instrument Exercise 3

The next step is to displace the downbeat's pulse to other parts of the bar. Imagine and practice the excerpt with the metronome sounding on the second beat of every bar, as follows:

EXAMPLE 2.95

This strengthens the rhythmic imagination. There are two stages to this step. The first stage is to tangibly feel the pulse on the two of each bar, making sure you line up perfectly with the metronome, and the second stage is to actually change the bar line.

Metronome and Instrument Exercise 4

Now shift the bar line. Feel it as follows:

EXAMPLE 2.96

The first E♭ now comes on beat *two*. This may seem strange at first. Don't worry; you won't lose the feeling for the real downbeat when you come back to it. Doing this will strengthen your rhythmic imagination and will ultimately help with the phrasing of the excerpt.

Metronome and Instrument Exercise 5

Now repeat the process with the pulse on the third beat of every bar:

EXAMPLE 2.97

Make sure you really line up with the metronome, especially on the tied notes in the fourth and fifth full bars. By that I mean, feel it particularly strongly there. Tied notes, and notes you don't play, are where you need to feel the pulse the most.

Metronome and Instrument Exercise 6

Feel the downbeats as follows:

EXAMPLE 2.98

The melody now starts on the downbeat, no pickup, which feels very strange.

Metronome and Instrument Exercise 7

Now shift your attention to the 16th-note pulse. Listen to the metronome set to 180, an octave above the eighth-note pulse. Memorize this pulse, imagine the piece listening to this pulse, and practice with the metronome set as follows:

EXAMPLE 2.99

Make sure every 32nd note comes exactly in-between the metronome clicks, and that the B♭ in the fifth bar lines right up with the pulse.

Take some time to practice with claves. Put your instrument down, pick up the claves, and see if you can play the abstract rhythm of the excerpt with the claves, hiding the metronome. (By abstract, I mean take the excerpt out of the realm of pitch, and play it purely as a rhythm.) Then, go back to your instrument, and see if that gave more clarity, solidity, and transparency to your playing, By transparency, I mean that while you are playing, you can see and feel through the notes to concentrate also on the pulse, or on other players, the ensemble, or what have you, detaching yourself from your own playing and being aware of other things.

Metronome and Instrument Exercise 8

Next comes every other 16th, setting the metronome to coincide with the "ands," creating a displaced pulse unison.

EXAMPLE 2.100

This is a terrific way to practice. The inner rhythm of the piece jumps out at you. Notice that at this setting the only note that falls with a metronome click is that D♭ in the fifth bar. That note becomes the rhythmic focus of the whole excerpt.

Metronome and Instrument Exercise 9

The next step is the smaller units of time, here the 32nd notes. Practice every excerpt in this way, hearing and feeling the smallest subdivision.

EXAMPLE 2.101

Line everything up. You may have to slow the metronome down to be able to really hear and concentrate on the smallest subdivisions. There is nothing wrong with that—in fact, it's extremely helpful to slow the tempos down—way down—when practicing excerpts. You could set the 32nd notes to 90 (which slows the tempo down two octaves). This is great practice in measured doses. Many people believe the best practice is done at exactly one-half the performance tempo, down one octave. In this case, that would be 32nd notes at mm=180.

As long as we're talking about slowing the metronome down, let's touch on speeding it back up again. Many people start at half tempo, and go through the excerpt (with no mistakes) time after time, moving the metronome up a bit every time, so it takes 10 to 20 repetitions to reach performance tempo. This is great practice. Be careful, though, that your playing doesn't develop a feeling of always going somewhere, getting faster, pushing the tempo up. Try "warming down"—that is, once you reach your fastest tempo, slow the metronome down bit by bit back to where you started. You may find it even harder to be accurate when getting slower.

Another alternative to moving the metronome to progressively faster tempos is to start at the middle and work both ways. First practice this excerpt at mm=60, then at 56, then at 66, then at 52, then at 72, then at 50, then at 80, then at 46, then at 90. Work progressively faster and slower at the same time. Then you can work backward in the same increments, to meet in the middle again, at 60.

Metronome and Instrument Exercise 10

The next step is to displace the metronome to the second 32nd of each beat, as follows:

EXAMPLE 2.102

You don't have to like every metronome displacement as much as another. This setting may feel a bit jumpy. But it's good for the concentration, and for feeling the internal rhythm.

Metronome and Instrument Exercise 11

EXAMPLE 2.103

Setting the metronome to the last 32nd note of each beat brings the character of all those 32nd-note pickups to the fore. Once you can play every one exactly right you then can make them slightly not right, if you desire. That's where character and expression come in. When you have awareness and control of the exact metronomic rhythm you can go on to subtly shape it.

Note that in playing the last two, as well as example 2.100, you are playing the basic eighth-note pulse, mm=90, but displacing it to various parts of the beat. Thinking in this manner helps you perform smoothly; you can let go of "placing" each note in its proper place, and get into playing the pulse, just displaced.

Metronome and Instrument Exercise 12

As long as we are displacing, try to displace the 32nd-note pulse onto every other 64th note.

EXAMPLE 2.104

This one is a pain to get right, but it really gets your mind clicking. Slow down the click.

You can also practice with a metronome set to all the 64ths, but that gets a little noisy. Slow way down and try it.

Metronome and Instrument Exercise 13

The final suggestion for this excerpt is harder to accomplish. It is to set the metronome to every other bar line, the double slow pulse, down three octaves. It's another important way to feel this excerpt. With this setting, the "question-answer" or "strong-weak" aspect of this theme comes out—in other words, the two-bar phrase.

EXAMPLE 2.105

This is at mm=15! The only metronome I know of that goes that slow is the one I'm developing. Another way to produce such a click is to make a recording of a pulse at mm=15 by turning the volume up and down every other beat while recording a pulse at mm=30. This is a challenging, rewarding click track to work with.

There are still other ways to set up the click, including:

1. Displace the last example, a beat every six eighth notes, in various ways.
2. Practice the excerpt in 6/8. In this case, set the click at 145. (In this excerpt, practicing in 6/8 doesn't feel right, but in many pieces in three it is terrific, as in the scherzo from Mendelssohn's *Midsummer Night's Dream,* or so many Bach pieces.)
3. Displace the 6/8 various ways.
4. Change the 32nds to triplets, or to 64ths (sometimes called practicing in rhythms).

Now move on to another external source for improving pulse and rhythm: the world of recording yourself, with and without a metronome.

Improving Pulse and Rhythm Through Recording

Recording and listening back to your own playing is the best way to get honest feedback. The recording doesn't lie. Listen to yourself often.

(There is a slight caveat regarding the statement that the recording doesn't lie. Sometimes a tape plays back at a slightly different speed than what you recorded. If you have any doubts, check your system by recording a metronome pulse, and then compare the recorded pulse with the metronome. It can also change the tone color. But even with these little distortions, the truth about your playing shows up clearly.)

Use the best equipment available, the simpler the better. The basics are a tape recorder and a metronome. Find a good metronome with a clear and pleasing sound, and one that phrases, if possible. A recorder that can go at half tempo is helpful for scrutinizing your playing, and necessary for some projects. Two- or four-track capabilities are also helpful.

Recording Exercise 1: Recording Yourself Playing a Pulse

Set your metronome to 80, and listen to it for a while. Imagine yourself playing the pulse. Turn off the metronome, and record yourself playing the pulse with your claves.

Before you even listen to it, notice how you feel, and how you felt playing it. Was it easy? Did your mind wander? If you pay attention to your feelings, you can fix problems before they happen.

Now listen to the recording. Is it smooth, even, solid and "fat"? Could you play along with it? Are you satisfied? (Hopefully you will never be entirely satisfied, in that it will never be absolutely perfect; you'll always be striving to improve.) Incorporate the chest pulse, your breathing; click your teeth if you need to. Find your own way to perform a steady pulse.

Progressively move the tempo of the metronome down over time. The slower you go, the harder it is.

It may make it easier to hold a steady pulse if you group the notes.

Recording Exercise 2: Phrasing in Groups of Notes

Try the following phrasings of two, three, four, and five, with "soft" accents:

EXAMPLE 2.106

Does the tempo push or drag toward and away from the accents? Where do the flams happen?

Take any excerpt you are working on. Perform and record the appropriate pulse, and practice with it. How does that feel? How can you make the recorded pulse easier to practice with?

Record in the same phrases as above, but now crescendo and diminuendo to each accent.

Record longer pulse phrases. Improvise, using dynamics, while holding a steady pulse. Listen back. Does the time distort when the volume changes? When you play an accent? Before or after an accent? Pay attention to your tendencies.

Try recording the metronome exercises from earlier in the book. Push your standard higher.

Recording Exercise 3: Playing Along with Metronome or Drum Machine Pulse Patterns

Create and practice to rhythmic patterns using shifting accents and rests performed by a metronome or drum machine. Here are a few suggestions:

Record a pulse with rests in it. The purpose of this is to play along with a metronome pulse, but have the metronome disappear for progressively longer periods of time. You have to maintain an inner pulse when the metronome disappears.

To record a metronome pulse with rests in it, you need to either use a metronome with which you can moderate the volume from full to off without altering the pulse, or you can turn the "record" level on the recording device to zero and back up at the appropriate moments.

Set the metronome to 120 and record the following. If you have a drum machine, you can just program it to perform the following patterns.

EXAMPLE 2.107

When practicing with that feels easy, record the following:

EXAMPLE 2.108

Be right with the metronome when it comes back in.

Record the following patterns, and practice the same way:

EXAMPLE 2.109

EXAMPLE 2.110

EXAMPLE 2.111

EXAMPLE 2.112

Make up patterns along these lines that work for you. Practice keeping a pulse with these patterns. Challenge yourself with progressively slower tempos. Record patterns at mm=100, 80, 60, and 40. If you can play along with the metronome sounding eight and silent for eight at mm=40, you are doing very well.

Use these patterns, metronome pulses with "holes," as templates for practice. Try all the metronome exercises with them. Practice your excerpts with them. Find like-minded friends and practice in ensemble with them. It is revealing and helpful to keep track of how you keep time during the silences. This is great work for drummers.

Recording Exercise 4: Recording Pulse Patterns and Counts

Another way to use mechanical pulse machines is to program or record a pulse with accent patterns or counting superimposed.

If you have a one-track recording machine, the routine is:

1. Pick the tempo at which you want to practice.
2. Set the metronome to the fastest subdivision.
3. Turn it on and leave it on.
4. Turn on your recorder.
5. Count a preparatory bar, and then count out the entire excerpt.

You then have a phrased pulse track, with you counting on it, to practice with. This is particularly helpful in music that has complex rhythms and meter changes, such as the excerpt from the end of Stravinsky's *Rite of Spring* on the following pages.

EXAMPLE 2.113 Excerpt from Stravinsky's *Rite of Spring*

Excerpt from Stravinsky's *Rite of Spring* (continued)

With a two-track machine:

1. Record the pulse on one track.
2. Record the count on the second track.

With three-track capabilities, you can practice with the pulse, the count, and the abstract rhythm of one part.

1. Record the metronome on one track.
2. Record the count on the second track.
3. Record the accents, or the rhythm of one particular part, on the third track.

With four tracks, you can record the pulse, the count, and the abstract rhythm of *two* parts. The examples on pages 2 ▪ 44 and 2 ▪ 45 demonstrate the benefits of this method.

One important advantage of two-, three-, and four-track capabilities is that you can adjust the relative volume of each part, depending on how you want to study. You can practice first listening to the pulse, the count, and the underlying accents, then pull the count out, then pull the pulse out, leaving just the accents.

Here is the routine for the bass part to the ending of *Rite of Spring*. The top line is to be played with claves; it is the abstract rhythm extracted from the bass part. The middle line is the count, the changing meter, and the bottom is the metronome pulse that goes evenly through the whole thing. Record them all.

EXAMPLE 2.114

Once you have created this Stravinsky pulse recording, practice along with your main instrument.

Going through this process serves two purposes: (1) by making the recording, you become intimate with the metric structure of this section, and (2) you then have a terrific "phrased pulse" of the excerpt to practice with. This gets you deep into the feel of the piece.

Now do the same routine for the viola part, from the exact same section at the exact same tempo:

EXAMPLE 2.115

If you are a viola player, you can play with this recording. But even better, if you are a bass player, play with this recording and feel how your part interlocks with the viola. Similarly, if you are a viola player, record the bass part in the abstract rhythm, as above, and practice with that. You fit into the holes of each other's part. These two rhythms are almost mirror images of each other.

No matter which instrument you play, you can practice with various recorded pulse patterns.

If you have a programmable drum machine, you can program it to perform the pulses outlined, and you can set it to practice with at various tempo markings. While programming a drum machine may seem easier, it is good to go through the metronome process outlined previously. This process promotes a clear understanding of the pulse and rhythm of the music, and helps you to easily perform the rhythms and changing meters in good time. Making a phrased pulse click track is time well spent as it helps to familiarize you with a piece. It can also prove especially helpful when learning complex contemporary music.

Recording Exercise 5: Checking Your Accuracy Against a Metronome

To check your rhythmic accuracy, it helps to play a metronome while listening back to your playing.

Take any excerpt. Decide on a tempo, set the metronome, and play your excerpt. Turn off the metronome, and turn on the recorder. Count one or two bars aloud, and play the excerpt.

Listen back. By lining up the metronome with your verbal count before the excerpt, you can hear whether or not you are holding the tempo perfectly.

You can also see if your counting, not just your playing, is in time. It is revealing to see how different counting tempo and playing tempo might be. Take some time to practice and simply record counting, while turning on and off the metronome, or counting using the "templates" outlined in Recording Exercise 3 on pages 2▪40 and 2▪41—that is, pulses with rests in between. Count through the rests. You may be surprised to find that your counting is often not at the same tempo as your playing or your thinking. Mastering accurate counting is critically important.

Recording Exercise 6: Listening to Yourself in General

You don't necessarily need a metronome to hear what you are doing rhythmically. Record yourself without a metronome. Then listen back to yourself, conduct or tap the time, or make some rhythmic motion. How does it feel? Strive to play the excerpt in such a way that it is nice and easy to move to and keep time with.

Tap your knees with your hands or fingers at the fastest pulse (the 32nds in the case of Metronome Exercises Part 2, the "Andante" in Beethoven's Fifth Symphony). It's easy to feel when the notes speed up or slow down. Notice when you have to adjust. Is it in the crescendos? The ends of phrases? Always on the dominant or appoggiatura? The hard spots? Become aware of it.

Listen with a friend, and listen to other people's tapes as well. Listening with and to others can reveal rhythm issues—and some of your own habits and tendencies—you hadn't previously considered.

Recording Exercise 7: Checking Your Rhythm at Half Speed

A tape machine that goes at half speed can be a great tool. Record your practice with a metronome going, and when you listen back at half speed, the moments where you "come apart" from the pulse—the flams, where you speed up and slow down—become easy to hear and analyze. The tempo fluctuations will jump out at you. Invest in a recorder that can play back at half tempo.

Recording Exercise 8: Multiple-Track Recording

A fun and revealing activity is to play duets with yourself. If you have a recorder with multiple-track capabilities, you can record a Bach, a Mozart, or any duet with yourself, as follows:

Count off and record part one on track one. Then, using headphones, record part two on track two while listening back to part one.

This is great practice, and fun to do. Performing rubatos, accelerandos, crescendos, and other expressive techniques with yourself forces you to think clearly and execute them well.

It is also helpful to perform simple pulse exercises with yourself. On one track of a two-track recorder, play a pulse, as evenly as possible. On the other track, record a displaced pulse unison. Listen back and see if it is a strong pulse, one with which you could practice. If not, keep working on it.

Record all the metronome exercises in this manner, practicing with your own pulse.

With a four-track recorder you can record yourself playing all four parts in a quartet. Playing it with rhythmic accuracy without a metronome can be a challenge—one worth working on.

You can also practice a simple pulse exercise with four parts, as follows:

On track one, record a slow metronome pulse, at mm=40 or so, for about a minute. Then listen back, subdividing each beat into four. Record, using headphones, beat two on track two, beat three on track three, and beat four on track four, as follows:

EXAMPLE 2.116

1 minute

Track 1, metronome

Track 2

Track 3

Track 4

All four tracks are the same pulse, displaced by a beat. Listening back, you can clearly hear your tendencies. If you hear a strong pulse when listening back, you are doing great. This isn't easy to do.

Try the above subdividing the slow pulse in different ways. Track one can be the downbeat for 4/4, 3/4, 6/8, and so on. Record different parts of the bar on different tracks.

Try subdividing the metronome pulse by two on track two, by three on track three, and by four on track four. Record all three parts listening only to the metronome track. Then listen back and see how your two-over-three-over-four rhythm sounds.

EXAMPLE 2.117

Do this one with rests in the rhythms, changing rhythms, trying quintuplets and beyond. Improvise. Use the imagination. This pulse recording routine helps to uncover your rhythmic tendencies.

If you can find a metronome with which you can modulate the tempo while it is playing, record a pulse that gently changes tempo. Record a displaced unison with the recorded track, subtly changing tempo with the metronome. Practice with a changing pulse; see how that feels. This is great for developing rhythmic flexibility and rubato. Adjusting to fluctuating pulse can help in your playing with other musicians.

Before talking about playing with other musicians, we should look at another recorded resource for improving rhythm: the radio and recordings of music.

Improving Pulse and Rhythm Using the Radio and Recordings

Listen, listen, and listen. Listen to the same piece over and over, listen to various recordings, and go to concerts. Develop your awareness of rhythm by broadening the range of music you listen to.

Both the radio and recordings are good resources. The advantages of the radio are its convenience, its element of surprise, and the exposure to music you might not listen to otherwise. The disadvantages are interruptions—mainly in the form of commercials—and the lack of control.

Turning the volume up and down is a good way to work on pulse. Choose a piece of music that has a strong pulse. Turn down the volume every other bar, and keep the music going in your head. Turn the volume back up after a bar, and see if you are still in time. Try it for two bars, or for four. If you have an easy-to-use volume control on the radio in your car, you can do it while stuck in traffic.

Use the radio to hear good music from all over the world. The more rhythms you are exposed to, the better.

Listen to different recordings of the same piece. You can learn a lot from noticing different performance practices, especially different tempos. Before you put on a recording, think of the tempo, and see if you can get it right on. See if you can perform different tempos of the same piece by remembering different recordings. Listen many times over to recordings you like.

Memorizing Tempos

Memorize tempos. Keep track somewhere of tempos of favorite recordings and tunes. You can use the pulses of particular tunes to recall particular tempos. You can memorize metronome marks by recalling performances of your favorite pieces.

Once you have one tempo memorized, you can access many tempos by doubling, halving, or subdividing in triplets. Using this systematic approach, you can access at least eight mm from each memorized tempo. Accomplish this with a few different pieces at a few various tempos, and you can "call up" virtually any desired tempo.

For example, take mm=120—march tempo. If you can recall "The Stars and Stripes," you can access mm=120. By halving that tempo you hear mm=60, and by doubling it you hear mm=240. If you feel the mm=60 half-time march pulse, you can subdivide it by three and feel mm=180. Then, remembering that pulse, you can half the mm=180 to feel a mm=90, and then again for mm=45 (going down by octaves). Remembering the 120 pulse, you can play dotted quarters, or a two against three, (*one* two *and* three) to feel mm=80. Double that pulse to hear mm=160, or halve it to access mm=40. With this system, you can call up mm=40, 45, 60, 80, 90, 120, 160, 180, and 240, from just remembering one march tempo. This is called good *relative click,* just as the ability to call up any pitch relative to A-440 is called good relative pitch.

Perfect click, like perfect pitch, is the ability to call up any pulse tempo with no reference whatsoever. Perfect click, like perfect pitch, remains a mystery to me.

Improving Pulse and Rhythm Through Interaction with Others

Musical experiences from real life are the most natural sources of rhythm practice. From your experiences as a child, singing and banging on pots and pans, through later involvement in bands, choirs, and orchestras; through improvising, rehearsing, performing, and going to concerts and live music; and through training with teachers, playing with and listening to others is basic. The world is and always has been the primary classroom.

Go to concerts. Pay attention to how various musicians and conductors feel time. Emulate players with good time. Improve through imitation.

Outside of your many musical projects, find like-minded musicians who want to work on time and pulse. The following are a few suggestions.

With Others Exercise 1

Simply play a pulse together. Take turns being leader and follower. The leader can pick up the tempo, slow down, play accents and meters, and change grooves, while the follower follows as closely as possible.

With Others Exercise 2

Play displaced pulse unisons with each other. Keep a tempo; speed up and slow down. See how fast you can go. Phrase pulse unisons and displaced pulse unisons in threes, fives, sevens, and nines. Displaced pulse unisons are great practice; it's like working on intonation.

With Others Exercise 3

Play all of this book's metronome exercises with a partner.

With Others Exercise 4

Record each other. Listen to recordings of exercises and music with each other. Critique and support each other.

With Others Exercise 5

Rehearse ensemble with a metronome going.

With Others Exercise 6

Play drums together (see "Hand Drumming," page 2▪54).

Improving Pulse and Rhythm Using Nature and Aspects of Daily Life

Rhythm is everywhere. Be sensitive to it, and stay aware of spontaneous occurrences that can spur rhythmic development. Listen all the time and use your imagination. Become a rhythm antenna.

If you're at the beach, hear the rhythm of the waves. How regular or irregular is it? Subdivide the rhythms you hear.

Listen to birdcalls. Memorize one and use it as a rhythmic inspiration for study. Crickets have great rhythm. Cats purr, dogs pant, horses gallop in time.

Wind creates rhythm, with flags, loose windows, leaves, and just by itself. Waterfalls have a steady rhythm.

You can hear random occurrences around the house in time, as an interesting rhythm. Let sounds fall into an imaginary time grid that you create. Set an inner pulse, and be aware of every sound you hear in relation to it.

Man-made objects can be good sources of rhythmic inspiration. If that drip from the waterspout is keeping you up, turn it into rhythmic phrases, subdivide it, improvise with it. Windshield wipers, washing machines, photocopiers, and internal combustion engines often provide great grooves. Riding on a train is a rhythmic experience. Telephones—feel the rhythm of the rings. Listen to the busy signal, and get the pulse. When you leave your phone off the hook, after the recording says "If you'd like to make a call, please hang up and dial again," there comes a long series of irritating beeps. Organize those beeps into groups of three, five, seven, and nine. They won't bother you quite as much.

When putting gas in the car, pay attention to the rate of the numbers going by. Feel the pulse, watch and count to 10, close your eyes and count the next 10, then open your eyes and see if you're in time. Compare the rate of the gallons' flow to the amount of money owed—there's always an interesting polyrhythm there. Then, when driving the car, feel the pulse of the telephone poles going by, or the frequency of the lines in the asphalt.

See if you can feel the slow pulse of foghorns. Subdivide; see how high you can count between each sounding. While you're at it, see if you can identify the pitch.

The point of all this is that if you pay attention, if you are "on to" rhythm, there is always a rhythm to study, or be inspired by. The same applies to pitch: if you are trying to develop perfect or relative pitch, always be aware of the pitches occurring around you, from birds, car horns, ads, planes—everything. If you are so inclined, every moment can present an opportunity for growth.

IMPROVING PULSE AND RHYTHM THROUGH MOTION AND ACTION

Moving in time is what rhythm is all about. Physical activities are rhythmic resources. To move is to groove.

Walking

Long walks are great for rhythm. There is a reason so many composers like walking. As you walk, rhythms and tunes naturally enter your imagination. As well as just letting this happen, you can consciously help it happen.

As you walk, pay attention to the rhythm of your steps, the phrasing of your stride. Hear the sound of your clothes rustling, your shoes scuffling. A great 6/8 can occur with your shoes shuffling along with your steps, while your arms brushing against keys in your pocket produce a jingling counter rhythm. Your arms, swinging in this manner, can be the pendulums of your internal clock.

Incorporating the breath creates other rhythms.

Be sensitive to the tempo of the steps. Feel the tempo slow down when you hit sand or go uphill, speed up when you hit asphalt or go downhill. This can become a tangible metaphor when you need to speed up or slow down in performance.

Subdivide your steps; create rhythms in your imagination. Perform musical excerpts in your mind at the tempo of your walking, whether it is the right tempo for the music or not. Then imagine the excerpt at the correct tempo, but keep walking at another tempo. This takes some mental control.

Jogging and Running

Running is highly rhythmic. Exploit it. All the same principles of walking occur when jogging, but at different energy levels, and with a different groove. The strides have a stronger physical pulse. The heartbeat comes more into play, and the breath comes stronger and faster. Again, be sensitive to all your body's rhythms of motion. Create polyrhythms among your breath, your strides, and your imagination. Organize your steps and run in different meters. Interact rhythmically with everything you pass. How many steps between each house, each pole, each block?

One fantastic source of interesting rhythms is chattering teeth. If you can stand to run or bike when very cold, lovely rhythms and polyrhythms occur from the teeth chattering while your legs are pumping and pulsing—fast odd times sometimes happen.

Riding a Bicycle

Settle into a groove while riding a bike. It's like walking or jogging, but the rhythm is smoother. Flexing the leg muscles gets the chest pulse going. Subdivide the cycles. Hear the sound of your clothes rustling, the cycle cycling, the drifting scenery, your breath in and out—everything's a moving rhythm. There's a steady pulse in the passing poles, and another in the broken line of the road. What's the polyrhythm between the two?

Sports in General

Every sport has its rhythm to master in order to play it well. Coordination in sports can help develop coordination in music. That isn't to say that you have to be a good athlete in order to play music well; many great musicians have played little in the way of sports. But it can help if you are open to it. (Just be careful of your hands and fingers!)

Some sports, including Ping Pong, tennis, racquetball, volleyball, basketball, and even pool, have more or less obvious rhythms. Sinking into the rhythm of the game will help your game and your rhythm.

Horseback riding is a rhythmic activity. It has all the advantages of walking, and your mind can really go free, sinking into the rhythms of the horse.

Use whatever sport you like.

Motion in General

Every once in a while, establish a rhythmic awareness of every little thing you do. Notice the rhythm of brushing your teeth, of picking up a cup and drinking it down, of shampooing in the shower, brushing hair, typing, cooking, gardening. Most are irregular rhythms, not periodic. But remember: every action has some rhythm.

Imagine a pulse underneath everything you do, as a kind of grid, to boost your consciousness of everyday rhythms. Doing this, you can become aware of interesting phrases in ordinary occurrences.

When on stage, every motion can relate to the music you're performing. Without making obvious gestures, you can tap into a subtle connection between the music you make and turning the page, or shifting your chair, or lifting your instrument. Sink into the music rhythmically surrounding you. Avoid overdoing bodily motions, especially tapping your feet or counting. It can attract attention and be a distraction to other musicians. Actions like these are only okay in the practice room—they can serve a valuable purpose there. But even in practice don't let them be crutches. Rely on your inner pulse; let your natural motions be at one with the music. Ensemble performance will benefit.

Body Music and Dancing

Another intriguing source of rhythm is called body music—the use of your body as an instrument, both by "playing your body" and by using your body to play non-musical instrument sources of sounds, like the wall or floor.

In the broadest sense, singing is body music. Although singing is rarely referred to that way, vocal sounds are a big part of body music.

Dancing is body music, though it usually takes a back seat to the music being danced to. In body music, the motion is part of the music. Tap dancing is truly body music, since the dancing creates the music being listened to. All dancing—especially tap dancing—is highly recommended.

You can create body music by clapping your hands, tapping the floor, taking steps, making sounds, tapping another person, thumping your chest while vocalizing—you name it. Any motion that makes a sound is fair game for body music.

There are worlds of rhythm the body can make. Create one rhythm by stepping in one pattern, a polyrhythm made by a different pattern of your hands on your chest, and a third by a vocal accompaniment. Take a body work class if you can; with others involved, a greater number of rhythm possibilities emerge.

Many world cultures link their music inextricably with body music. Bells around the ankles, used in Africa and other places, are body music. Cultures using dance as a part of music make body music. Singers like Bobby McFerrin, who use voice and body to produce a wide range of sounds, are using body music.

Dancing develops rhythm. Take a dance class, go out dancing; try any style, all styles. It's all good.

Hand Drumming

Drum. There is no better way into rhythm, pulse, time, and flow than to drum. Get together with like-minded players who want to drum, find some drums, and drum.

The following is a short course on hand drumming.

Drumming Step 1: Preparing to Play

Find a drum. Any drum larger than eight inches in diameter will do. A conga drum is ideal. Try to find a drum that doesn't have a rim extending higher than the drumhead, because as you play, your thumb can strike the rim, getting in the way and potentially hurting.

A standing position is best, although sitting is fine, too. Make sure there are no obstructions near the arms, so if you're sitting, use a chair without armrests.

Position yourself, if possible, so that the drumhead is somewhere around the level of your navel, so your hands can rest comfortably on the drumhead, with a slight angle down from your elbows to your hands.

Drumming Step 2: Hand and Finger Positions

Rest both hands on the drumhead. Place your hands so that the palm just below the fingers is resting on the edge of the drum. The fingers rest on the drumhead. The thumbs are relaxed, resting on the drum edge or just outside the edge.

Stay in this position for a while without playing, just focusing your attention on your arms, shoulders, neck, and back. Make sure everything is relaxed. Feel the weight of your arms resting on the drum.

Drumming Step 3: Flexing the Fingers

Just lift your fingers while keeping your palms in contact with the head, and while keeping the weight of the arms resting on the head; that is, stretch the fingers off the head for a moment, and then release them back onto the head, without lifting the hands from the rim. Do this a few times. Feel the muscles used in this small motion—no tension, just a stretch. This allows the fingers to bounce and stay off the head, while the arms are relaxed and the hands are resting on the rim. This little finger stretch will allow a nice tone to emerge from the drum.

Drumming Step 4: Dropping the Hand

Drop your weak arm down by your side and keep your strong arm in contact with the drum.

Lift your entire hand a few inches off the drumhead, and let it flop back onto the head. Don't worry about the tone yet, nor the pulse. Just concern yourself with the act of dropping or flopping the hand onto the drum, with no force or tension. Do it a few times, paying attention to the feeling in your hand, elbow, arm, shoulders, and neck, keeping everything loose and relaxed. Don't hit, just drop, as if you were flopping a dead fish on the block. This produces a muffled tone.

When you feel comfortable with this dropping motion, stretch the fingers a bit so they come up a little, right at the moment of contact. If you time this light finger tension at the right moment, just when the hand flops onto the head, a nice open tone will occur. The fingers rebound off the head, but the palm just below the fingers does not come off the edge of the head. This allows for a very relaxed technique: you drop the hand on, and just let the fingers rebound a bit—you don't have to lift the whole hand and arm into the air after striking to create a nice tone. This technique helps to avoid smashing into the drum.

Note the curving up of the fingers as the strong hand drops on the drum. Try it next with the weak hand. Just drop it on, letting the fingers bounce off.

When you have produced an open tone with both hands by themselves, begin alternating hand strokes, right and left, back and forth, not yet worrying about time or pulse. Pay attention to the tone being produced, and give yourself feedback. Notice what happens if you drop the hand from different heights, at different speeds, with different feelings. Pay attention always to the tone being produced. When you hear a nice tone, be aware of how you produced it. Go for a nice, big, open tone. You want the right and left hands to sound the same.

The symbol for this open tone is an O above the note.

Listen to the sound produced when you do *not* exert that slight finger tension at the moment of contact. It's a muffled tone. This is also a good sound, a timekeeping sound, which contrasts with the open sound.

The symbol for this muffled tone is –, a line, or no symbol at all.

Drumming Step 5: Dropping the Hands in Time

Begin alternating strokes in time. Go slow enough to pay attention to all the muscles, from your fingers through your shoulders, with every stroke.

EXAMPLE 2.118

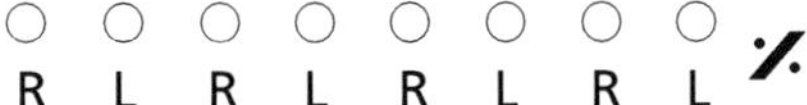

Lead with your strong hand. All of the following drum exercises are strong-hand led. Therefore, if you are left-handed, switch the symbols, and start with your strong (left) hand.

Once you can produce a series of similar-sounding open tones, think about time. Engage in a strong pulse, at a comfortable rate, and produce a series of nice open tones in good time.

Drumming Step 6: Muffle Pulse

Step six is the same as step five, but with muffled tones. Let the hand and fingers flop on and stay in contact with the head. Get used to producing a series of muffled tones, and when you can produce a series of even muffled tones, do it in good time.

EXAMPLE 2.119

R L R L R L R L

Drumming Step 7: Mixing Open and Muffled Tones

The next step is to start mixing up open and muffled tones to create rhythms. At first you'll find that you have to consciously raise the left hand early when producing an open tone with the right, and vice versa, in order for the open tone to ring. As you get comfortable with drumming, this will become automatic, and the lifting will become more subtle and unconscious. Staying relaxed helps this process.

Start with the following rhythm:

EXAMPLE 2.120

You can create infinite patterns using just open and muffled tones. From here you can go anywhere.

Getting the open tone with the weak hand is important for syncopation and freedom in phrasing. This is the famous "Bo Diddley beat," my favorite for getting started with incorporating the weak hand:

EXAMPLE 2.121

Play in 3/4 time. Here's a nice, basic three:

EXAMPLE 2.122

```
|: O  _  O  _  _  O | O  _  O  _  _  O :|
   R  L  R  L  R  L | R  L  R  L  R  L
```

Improvise, make up beats—the possibilities are endless. Once you are more or less comfortable playing in simple time, in 3/4 and 4/4, go on to compound time. Start with a simple 6/8:

EXAMPLE 2.123

```
6     12  O  _  _  O  _  _  O  _  _  O  _  _ :|
8  or  8  R  L  R  L  R  L  R  L  R  L  R  L
```

6/8 is excellent because it involves the weak hand in the main pulse. For drumming in compound time, the weak and strong hand become more balanced. Compound time opens up the world of polyrhythms, where playing with others takes on another level of depth.

Let's move right into 12/8. A good starting tempo is dotted quarter = 80-100.

In 12/8, one person plays pattern 2.123 above, which becomes now a 12/8. Another plays the following:

EXAMPLE 2.124

```
12  O  _  O  _  O  _  O  _  O  _  O  _ :|
 8  R  L  R  L  R  L  R  L  R  L  R  L
```

These two rhythms create a two over three, which you can also feel as a four over six.

Bring in a third player playing the following:

EXAMPLE 2.125

```
12  O  _  _  _  O  _  _  _  O  _  _  _ :|
 8  R  L  R  L  R  L  R  L  R  L  R  L
```

This creates a simple three over four.

The next line, for a fourth player, is sometimes called the African clave, usually played on cowbell using the rhythm of the open tones.

EXAMPLE 2.126

```
12  O     O     O  O     O     O     O :|
 8  R  L  R  L  R  L  R  L  R  L  R  L
```

If player three puts in an open sound with the L hand after every open tone with the R, you get:

EXAMPLE 2.127

```
12  ○  ○  —  —  ○  ○  —  —  ○  ○  —  — :||
 8  R  L  R  L  R  L  R  L  R  L  R  L
```

Which makes it funky.

Then, player one can shift one eighth, as follows:

EXAMPLE 2.128

```
12  —  ○  —  —  ○  —  —  ○  —  —  ○  — :||
 8  R  L  R  L  R  L  R  L  R  L  R  L
```

Which funkifies it further.

It's endless. Feel it in three and four at the same time. Keep going and make up your own.

Drumming Step 8: Adding Accents

The accent is one more important basic technique to discuss here. You can play all the rhythms outlined above using accents instead of open or muffled tones. You can also mix accents into the rhythms above, for more rhythmic shape. It is indicated with an accent mark: >.

You can accent either the muffled tone or the open tone simply by lifting the hand a bit higher and letting it drop from a higher position, or by pulling it off the head quicker. Both produce a louder sound. Avoid getting an accent by hitting harder. Better to think bigger, quicker, or higher.

Another way to accomplish an accent is to produce a higher, snappier tone, called the *slap*. To accomplish this, you exert some muscular control at the moment of contact with the drumhead, a kind of squeeze into the head. Instead of letting the fingers bounce off the head, as for the open tone, use the muscles to go *into* the head, to produce a slap. You feel like you're grabbing the head with your fingers. If it's done right, a snappy slap tone is produced.

Avoid pain. Superficial soreness in the hands is okay. You'll get over it and be able to keep drumming tomorrow or the day after. A blister is no big deal. But be vigilant about muscular soreness, or banging yourself. Don't hurt yourself. If your muscles or bones are starting to hurt, stop and analyze what you're doing. Don't play through pain (with any instrument). If you are drumming correctly, staying relaxed, and not "hitting" the drum, you shouldn't experience pain. Let your hands drop; don't hit. As you get better at letting the hands drop, you can begin to let them drop with some force, and you won't hurt yourself.

The slap is also indicated with an accent mark.

Here are a couple of 12/8 patterns incorporating the slap:

EXAMPLE 2.129

EXAMPLE 2.130

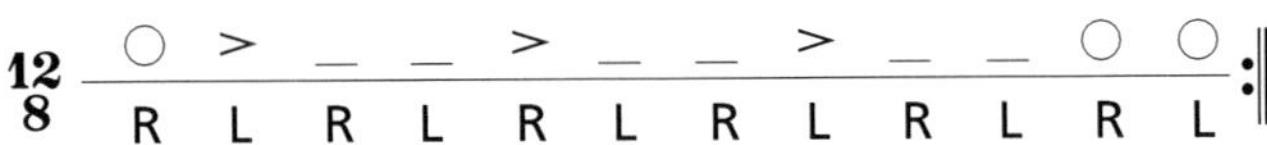

Drumming Step 9: Keep Going

Keep practicing, staying relaxed, improvising. Play grooves for extended periods of time. Get lost in it; feel hypnotized by it. Find some like-minded friends and make a drum circle. Get together with a drum teacher or facilitator, and keep at it. Play in different styles; play along with records in all styles and cultural traditions, especially African and Latin music. It feels great and the benefits are tremendous.

BOOK

3

Advanced Rhythm Studies

Advanced Rhythm Studies

Advanced Rhythm Studies covers material that professional musicians can expect to encounter in their careers, especially if they're involved in contemporary concert performance. This book also has material specifically for drumset players, and for those who want to delve more deeply into rhythmic studies. It is a good idea to have a strong grasp of the material presented in Book Two before delving into this book.

After studying the concepts presented here, you will be ready to tackle even the gnarliest polyrhythmic problems encountered in the contemporary literature.

ODD TIME SIGNATURES AND MIXED METER

Odd time signatures are meters in 5, 7, 9, 10, 11, 13, 14, 15, 17, and any number above. They are also called mixed meter, as they can result from adding meters together. Odd times are nothing new. The traditions of India, Eastern Europe, and other regions of the world use odd time signatures often and with ease. Those of us trained in the Western tradition may not be so used to them.

Expose yourself as much as possible to music that uses odd times and mixed meters. Listen to and study the music of India and Eastern Europe. There's great music in jazz and rock that employs odd times—for example, "Take Five" by the Dave Brubeck Quartet, "The Grunge" and other Led Zeppelin tunes, and the music of the Mahavishnu Orchestra and other fusion bands. Also, so much contemporary orchestral and chamber music is in odd times. Study it and watch the score go by, tapping your foot at the bar lines. Get used to it.

Mixed meter is just that. 5/4 time is usually three plus two or two plus three. The second movement of Tchaikovsky's sixth symphony is a gentle 5/4, phrased two plus three all the way through. Seven is usually four plus three or three plus four. Similarly, meters in 10, 11, 13, and so forth are broken up into groups of two, three, and four. Nine is either a compound meter of three groups of three or a mixed meter, as in "Rondo á La Turk" by Dave Brubeck, which is two plus two plus two plus three. A piece in eight can be mixed meter if it is organized into three plus two plus three. Salsa music based on the clave can be seen as mixed meter, as it is three plus three plus four plus two plus four.

Gain ease at advanced mixed meters. There are ways to practice that can make your practice time more productive and your performance easier and more musical. When you are challenged by a piece in odd time or mixed meter, analyze it and approach it as in as many ways as you can.

To start, let's look again at something that is not really an odd time, but a simple mixed meter: the rhythm extracted from "America" from Bernstein's *West Side Story*, mixing 6/8 and 3/4.

EXAMPLE 3.1

There's the hemiola again. It is an alternation between 6/8 and 3/4, two groups of three and three groups of two, also known as two over three.

When practicing this mixed meter, stay in touch with the steady big pulse occurring on each downbeat. The accents go lightly on top of this basic pulse.

The following are five suggestions for becoming fluent with this rhythm, starting with using the hands, as if drumming. These concepts can be applied to the study of all mixed meters.

1. First practice what's called the hand-to-hand method, hitting your legs or a desk or a drum, as follows:

   EXAMPLE 3.2

   Tap your foot or chest pulse on each downbeat.

   Keep the rhythm flowing along. If you feel yourself getting stuck on the accents, lighten them up. Try it slower. Play it without accents for a while, or just imagine the accents. Then return to performing them.

2. Practice the rhythm with your hands in the following manner, keeping the running eighth notes with one hand and the accents with the other:

   EXAMPLE 3.3

   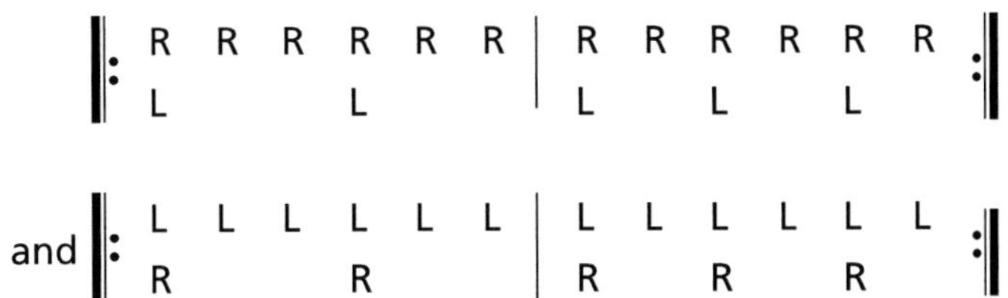

3. A third way to practice with your hands is to play this:

EXAMPLE 3.4

‖: R L L R L L | R L R L R L :‖
or L R R L R R | L R L R L R

4. Articulate the rhythm with nonsense syllables, like, for this one:

   "Diddle a diddle a diddle diddle diddle" or "ooh ka cha ooh ka cha ooh ka ooh ka ooh ka." Keep it light.

5. Practice it with the metronome clicking in various ways—on the downbeats, the dotted quarters, the quarters, and every other downbeat.

Fives Exercise

Fives are grouped as two plus three or three plus two. Practice them in the hand-to-hand method, as follows:

EXAMPLE 3.5

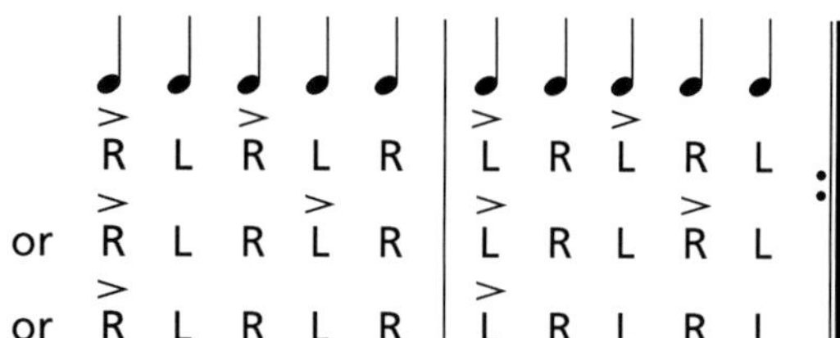

Also work on fives in the other ways outlined above.

The Planets by Gustav Holst (1894–1934) has some odd times. The opening movement, "Mars," is a 5/4 allegro that can feel like a "pure" five (not subdivided), with a heavy downbeat, but it is phrased in three plus two. Another point of interest in this movement is that it juxtaposes a triplet on the downbeat with the two eighths on beat four, so you get odd time and polyrhythm in every bar. The following is the famous rhythm extracted from the music, with three possible hand patterns written out.

EXAMPLE 3.6

Sevens Exercise

Sevens are usually grouped four plus three or three plus four. Get used to the feel using the following hand-to-hand study routine:

EXAMPLE 3.7

Nines Exercises

Nines are great to work with. Go through the nines outlined in the metronome exercises, finding hand patterns you like.

Bartók used mixed meter often, which makes sense because he came from a part of the world in which mixed meter is an everyday musical experience. His *Sonata for Two Pianos and Percussion* has many nine groupings. Here's the rhythm from the main theme:

EXAMPLE 3.8

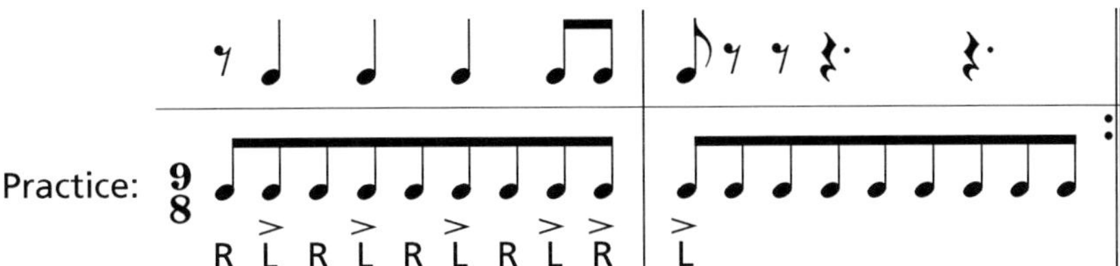

The following is a short study based on the rhythms in that piece. Getting used to rhythms like these seems to be a stumbling block for many musicians. Practice it in all the ways outlined above. If you can easily play through it at a good clip, keeping good time, you're coming along in the odd time world.

EXAMPLE 3.9

There are millions of them. Count, relax, and flow. After that, it's a matter of practice and building familiarity.

RHYTHMS IN CONTEMPORARY MUSIC: ADVANCED POLYRHYTHMS AND COMPLEX POLYRHYTHMIC CHANGES

We turn now to interpreting more difficult polyrhythms: how to play five over four, seven over three, nine over five, and beyond, and how to go back and forth between them. It's important to move logically and methodically from easier to more advanced. Once you get the hang of how to play the rhythms encountered here, you'll find it less difficult to play polyrhythmic passages by Stravinsky, Bartók, John Cage, Edgar Varèse, Elliott Carter, Frank Zappa, and other more contemporary composers.

There's a logical system for figuring out and playing all polyrhythms. It involves a little math, subdividing, counting, and keeping a strong pulse.

Polyrhythms involve two numbers: one is the number that is going *over* the other, and the other is the number that is being *overed* (which is usually but not always the meter of the piece).

There are two mathematical approaches for solving polyrhythms, two ways of looking at the same thing.

The first approach: Subdivide each beat in the bar into the number of subdivisions that are going "over" them, and then group the subdivisions into units of the second number, the one that is being "overed."

The second approach: Multiply the two numbers to find the lowest common multiple. Divide the bar into that lowest common multiple, and then group those divisions into units of the two numbers.

Clear as mud? It is not easy to explain verbally; it has to be done rhythmically. It will become clear by going through the process outlined below.

The starting point is the most fundamental polyrhythm, the hemiola—that is, three over two and two over three.

Two-over-Three Exercises

In 3/4 time, two over three can look like this:

EXAMPLE 3.10

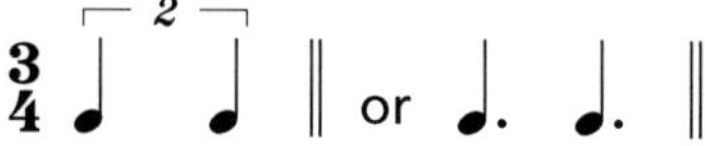

The bar is naturally divided into three quarter note pulses, by virtue of the time signature, but we are asked to perform two equal pulses in the same period. The polyrhythm is the two beats over the three quarters.

You accomplish that by first subdividing each quarter note of the bar by two, the number that is "over" the other. That gives eighths.

EXAMPLE 3.11

Then group those subdivisions into units of three, the number being "overed."

EXAMPLE 3.12

Play only the first note of each of group of three eighth notes, and there's your polyrhythm, two over three.

The second way of solving the simple two over three is: Determine the lowest common multiple of three and two, which is six. Divide the bar into six, which is done with eighth notes:

EXAMPLE 3.13

If you group the six eighths into two groups of three, you accomplish the two over three:

EXAMPLE 3.14

Get used to counting various ways.

Counting all the eighths, it is

1 2 3 4 5 6

Counting each beat and its subdivision, it is

1 + 2 + 3 +

or better for polymetric purposes:

1 2 **2** 2 **3** 2

Get used to the last way of counting. It works well for understanding and playing polyrhythms.

One way to count the two over three is:

1 2 3 **4** 5 6

Or, better for figuring out polyrhythms, count

1 2 2 **2** 3 2.

The accented numbers are the ones going "over" the other.

Three-over-Two Exercises

In 2/4 time, three over two can look like this:

EXAMPLE 3.15

You figure out how to play this by dividing each quarter into three, as follows:

EXAMPLE 3.16

You can count it like this:

one trip let two trip let, or one two three four five six

Or, better for our purposes,

1 2 3 **2** 2 3

Then you group this subdivision into three groups of two beats each (three over two):

EXAMPLE 3.17

Count:

one trip *let* two *trip* let,

or better,

1 2 **3** 2 **2** 3

and so accomplish the three over two.

Before going on to more complex polyrhythms, I want to interject four ways to use the hands to study polyrhythms.

Polyrhythm Hand Exercise 1

A good way to get used to polyrhythms is to practice with the two hands doing different things. One hand plays the fastest subdivisions (the lowest common multiple) and the other hand performs the specified groupings—in this case, the twos or the threes.

EXAMPLE 3.18

Play one pattern for a while, then the other. Then go back and forth, switching from three to two to three to two. Switch which hand plays the fast pulse and which hand plays the accents.

Polyrhythm Hand Exercise 2

Perform the following, called the hand-to-hand system, as used for odd-time study:

EXAMPLE 3.19

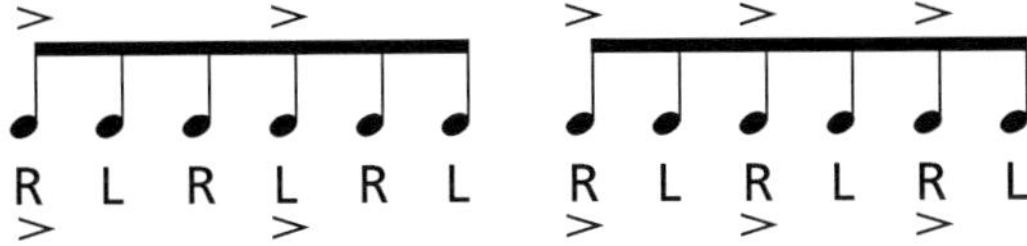

Polyrhythm Hand Exercise 3

Set the metronome to the downbeats, and perform the three, then the two, with both hands, as follows:

EXAMPLE 3.20

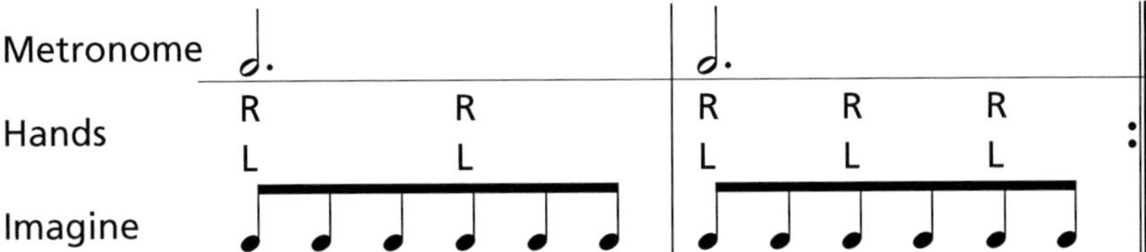

Polyrhythm Hand Exercise 4

The fourth way is to play both rhythms at the same time, one with the right, the other with the left, and then switch.

With the metronome playing the large beats, perform the following:

EXAMPLE 3.21

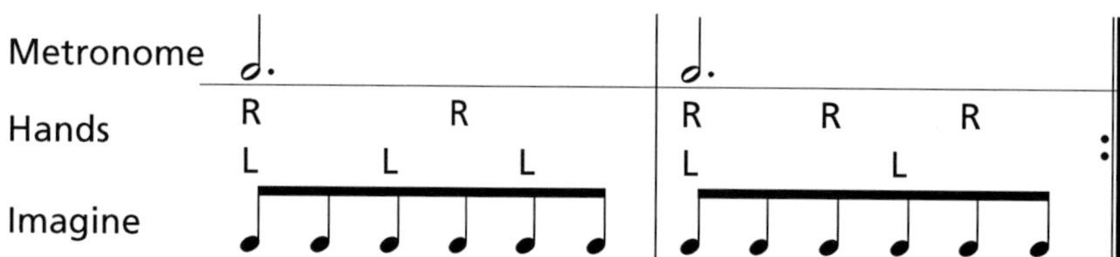

You can apply the preceding four hand exercises to every polyrhythm that follows.

Proceeding to a more complex polyrhythm, look at four over three and three over four.

Four-over-Three Exercises

In 3/4 time, four over three can look like this:

EXAMPLE 3.22

Performing this is accomplished by dividing the three quarters of the 3/4 into four beats each, yielding twelve 16th notes.

EXAMPLE 3.23

Then group these 16th-note subdivisions into units of three, the number being overed.

EXAMPLE 3.24

Play the first note of each group, and there's your four over three.

Counting it sounds like:

one e and *a* two e *and* a three *e* and a

Or better:

1 2 3 **4** 2 2 **3** 4 3 **2** 3 4

The numbers in boldface get the emphasis, and they are the four over the three.

There is always a pattern to the emphasized numbers, as outlined in all the examples that follow. The polyrhythm that is over the other *always shows up* in the emphasized numbers, but not necessarily in order—in this case, four shows up emphasized (one, four, three, and two) because it is *four* over three, but in backwards order.

The other system for solving this polyrhythm is to multiply four by three, making 12. Then divide the bar into 12 equal subdivisions, which is accomplished with 16ths. Then group the 16ths into groups of three, the number being overed, creating four units of three 16ths each.

Here is the process you go through to get to the polyrhythm:

EXAMPLE 3.25

Three-over-Four Exercises

In 4/4 time, three over four can look like the following, a half-note triplet:

EXAMPLE 3.26

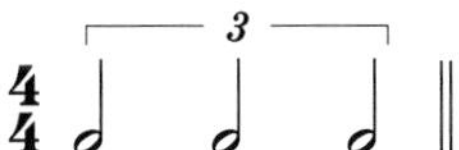

You accomplish this polyrhythm by dividing each beat, each quarter of the 4/4 bar, into three equal bits. By putting triplets to each beat, we have 12 triplet eighth notes, 12 being the lowest common multiple:

EXAMPLE 3.27

Counting it sounds like this:

one trip let *two* trip let *three* trip let *four* trip let

Or better:

1 2 3 **2** 2 3 **3** 2 3 **4** 2 3

By grouping this subdivision into four beats each, we accomplish the three over four:

EXAMPLE 3.28

Play the first note of each group, and you accomplish the three over four.

Counting sounds like

one trip let two *trip* let three trip *let* four trip let

Or better:

1 2 3 2 **2** 3 3 2 **3** 4 2 3

The emphasized numbers are the three over the four. In this case they come in order: one, two, three.

Here is the process you go through to get to the polyrhythm:

EXAMPLE 3.29

Good rhythmic performance often involves subdividing. It's necessary to subdivide to play this big triplet polyrhythm accurately, and subdividing helps to keep the pulse steady.

Practice this exercise for alternating between four and three:

EXERCISE 3.30

Practice first with the bars of rest, as shown, subdividing in your head during the rests. Then take out the bars of rests and accurately change from one to the other, with no rest in between.

Five-over-Four Exercises

In 4/4 time, five over four can look like this:

EXERCISE 3.31

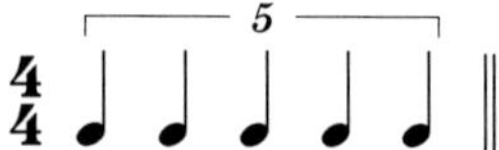

To perform it, subdivide the four quarters of the bar into five equal beats each, by using quintuplets. The total number of subdivisions of the bar now equals 20, the lowest common multiple of four and five.

EXERCISE 3.32

Group the notes into units of four small beats each:

EXERCISE 3.33

Counting it sounds like this:

Note the resulting count pattern, one through five, but backward from five to one. This is similar to the counting backward from four to one that occurs in four over three. The sooner you get used to these counting patterns, the easier the performance of polyrhythms becomes.

Here is the process you go through to get to the polyrhythm:

EXAMPLE 3.34

Four-over-Five Exercises

In 5/4 time, four over five can look like this:

EXAMPLE 3.35

To get this polyrhythm, divide the five quarters of the bar into four beats each, 16ths, accomplishing the subdivisions necessary for the lowest common multiple of four and five, which is 20.

EXAMPLE 3.36

Group the 16ths into units of five as follows:

EXAMPLE 3.37

Counting it sounds like this:

1 2 3 4 2 **2** 3 4 3 2 **3** 4 4 2 3 **4** 5 2 3 4

This time the counting pattern goes *up* from one to four.

Here is the process you go through to get to the polyrhythm:

EXAMPLE 3.38

Now try alternating between four and five, again with and without the rests.

EXAMPLE 3.39

Two-over-Five Exercise

In 5/4 time, two over five can look like this:

EXAMPLE 3.40

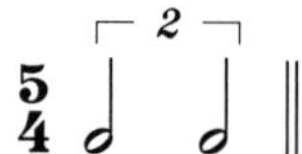

Divide each quarter of the 5/4 by two (eighth notes)—the number going "over"—creating 10 beats to the bar. Then group the eighths into groups of five, the number being "overed."

EXAMPLE 3.41

Counting it comes out:

1 2 2 2 3 **2** 4 2 5 2

Five-over-Two Exercise

In 2/4 time, five over two can look like the following:

EXAMPLE 3.42

By subdividing the quarters by quintuplets, we divide the bar into 10 beats, the lowest common multiple of five and two.

Grouping these subdivisions into units of two, we have:

EXAMPLE 3.43

Counted sounds like:

Note this counting pattern. Neither straight up nor down (numerically), it's jagged oscillation. But still, each member of the group of five comes only once, and five is the rhythm that goes over the other.

Three-over-Five Exercise

In 5/4 time, three over five can look like this:

EXAMPLE 3.44

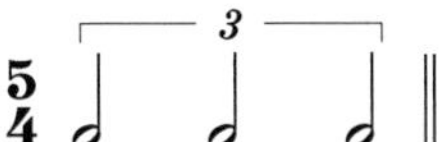

To play it, subdivide the five quarter notes in the bar into three beats each, giving 15 total beats, and group them into units of five:

EXAMPLE 3.45

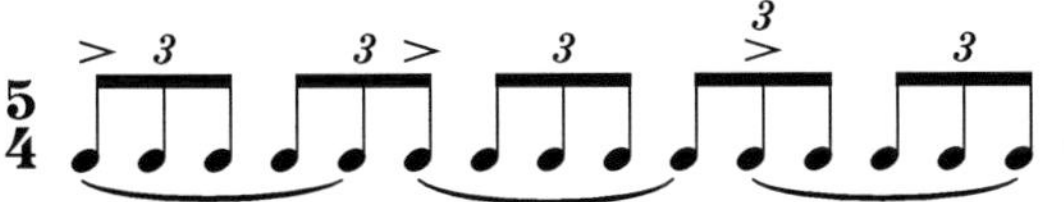

Counting it sounds like:

1 2 3 2 2 **3** 3 2 3 4 **2** 3 5 2 3

Five-over-Three Exercise

In 3/4 time, five over three can look like this:

EXAMPLE 3.46

For five over three, subdivide the quarters into quintuplets, and group them like this:

EXAMPLE 3.47

Counting it sounds like:

1 2 3 **4** 5   2 **2** 3 4 **5**   3 2 **3** 4 5

Alternating Two, Three, Four, and Five

Practice alternating twos, threes, fours, and fives. For practice set the quarter note to equal 35–100.

EXAMPLE 3.48

Practice each bar by itself, with and without rests, before you try this whole exercise. Then practice all the bars, both with and without rests, without stopping.

Now on to the sevens. We skip the sixes, as you can work with them using the same principles as the threes.

Four-over-Seven Exercise

In 7/4 time, four over seven can look like this:

EXAMPLE 3.49

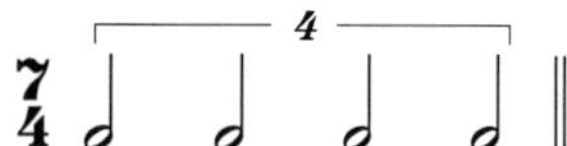

To perform four over seven, subdivide the seven quarters into 16th notes, and group these twenty-eight 16th notes into units of seven, as follows:

EXAMPLE 3.50

Counting it sounds like:

1 2 3 4   2 2 3 **4**   3 2 3 4   4 2 **3** 4   5 2 3 4   6 **2** 3 4   7 2 3 4

The big numbers in boldface produce the four over seven. Notice the pattern of counting backwards from four to one when you repeat this pattern. Every polyrhythm has a counting pattern associated with it.

Seven-over-Four Exercise

Seven over four can look like this:

EXAMPLE 3.51

Subdivide the beats into septuplets, and group every four, as follows:

EXAMPLE 3.52

Counting it sounds like this:

1 2 3 4 **5** 6 7   2 **2** 3 4 5 **6** 7   3 2 **3** 4 5 6 **7**   4 2 3 **4** 5 6 7

This pattern of counting is not as easy to see as the one for four over seven. While jagged, it is still a clear repetitive pattern that you can get used to with practice.

Alternating Four and Seven

Practice alternating fours and sevens.

EXAMPLE 3.53

Practice first with, then without, the rests.

Two-over-Seven Exercise

Two over seven can look like this:

EXAMPLE 3.54

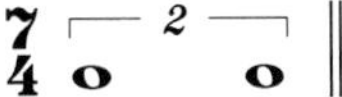

To perform it, subdivide the quarters of the bar into eighth notes and group them into two groups of seven as follows:

EXAMPLE 3.55

Counting it sounds like this:

1 2 2 2 3 2 4 **2** 5 2 6 2 7 2

The accented numbers are the polyrhythm, the two, which goes over the seven beats in the bar.

Seven-over-Two Exercise

Seven over two can look like this:

EXAMPLE 3.56

To perform it, subdivide the two quarters of the bar into septuplets, and group them into twos like this:

EXAMPLE 3.57

Counting it sounds like this:

1 2 **3** 4 **5** 6 **7** 2 **2** 3 **4** 5 **6** 7

This one can take a bit of practice, but is a very nice groove once you get used to it. Spend some time first getting used to counting seven to each beat.

Alternating Twos and Sevens

Practice alternating twos and sevens. For practice set the quarter note to equal 35–86.

EXAMPLE 3.58

Three-over-Seven Exercise

In 7/4 time, three over seven can look like this:

EXAMPLE 3.59

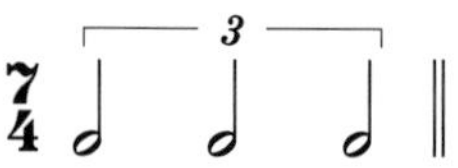

To perform it, subdivide the seven quarters of the bar into triplets, thereby accomplishing the lowest common multiple of three and seven, which is 21. Group the triplets into units of seven, as follows:

EXAMPLE 3.60

Counting it sounds like this:

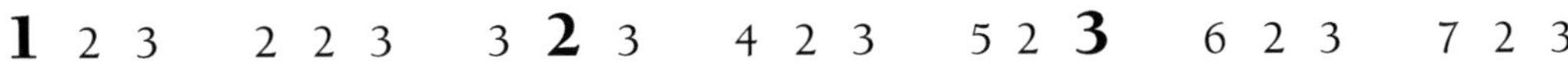

Seven-over-Three Exercise

In 3/2 time, seven over three can look like this:

EXAMPLE 3.61

To perform it, subdivide the three half notes of the bar into septuplets, accomplishing the lowest common multiple of 21, and group these subdivisions into groups of three, as follows:

EXAMPLE 3.62

Counting it sounds like this:

The accented numbers make the seven over the three.

Alternating Threes and Sevens

Practice alternating threes and sevens. For practice set the quarter note to equal 35–76.

EXAMPLE 3.63

Listen to the metronome for a while before going at this. Feel the large pulse strongly. Imagine the subdivisions, then perform, with then without the rests.

Continue this study as far as you can. Once you have the idea, you can figure out how to play any polyrhythm.

Higher Numbers

Once you get into the higher numbers than those we have worked on, five over six, seven over five or six, the sixes over sevens and 10s, and beyond, the subdivisions go by quickly. When the lowest common multiple is above 30 or so, you may get a better result by approximating it, by feeling it, rather than by doing the math. It gets too complicated, and it goes by too fast to allow perception of all the tiny subdivisions and accents, let alone try to count them all while performing the polyrhythm. The result becomes unmusical. Sometimes in music, just like sometimes in math, the best or most usable results are accomplished by approximation.

Before getting into approximation, though, there are many high numbers that you can "break down" by dividing them into smaller numbers, and get a good result. If one of the polyrhythms is an even number like six or eight, you can divide the number by two, and work out the polyrhythm quite exactly. Similarly, if one of the polyrhythm numbers is a compound number, 9 or 12 or 15, you can divide it by three, and gain good results that way.

Look at nines, for example. Nine is interesting because it is divisible by three equal groups of three. As I said in the last paragraph, when you get into the high numbers, it gets difficult to count. So when analyzing polyrhythms using nine, it is more successful to analyze them by subdividing by three, and then subdividing each of those beats by three, as follows:

Nine-over-Four Exercises

In 4/4 time, nine over four can look like this:

EXAMPLE 3.64

It can also look like this, with the nines grouped into three units of three beats each.

EXAMPLE 3.65

Whichever way it looks, it is easier to perform if you feel the three bigger beats over the meter of four, and simultaneously feel those three beats subdivided into three smaller beats, or triplets.

To get accustomed to this polyrhythm, use the following three steps.

EXAMPLE 3.66

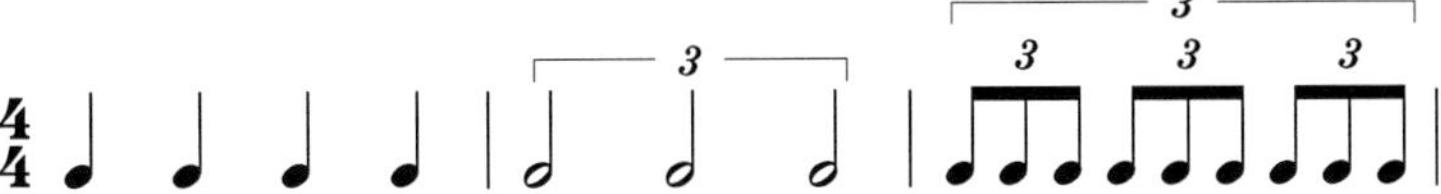

Practice this. Then drop the middle bar, and go straight from the four quarters to the nine.

Nine-over-Five Exercise

This is the same principle, but takes a bit more practice, or more familiarity with polyrhythms.

First review three over five, which we covered on page 3 ▪ 15.

Once you are used to feeling the relationship or the juxtaposition of three over five, you accomplish this polyrhythm by first feeling the big three over five, and then dividing each of those three into triplets.

EXAMPLE 3.67

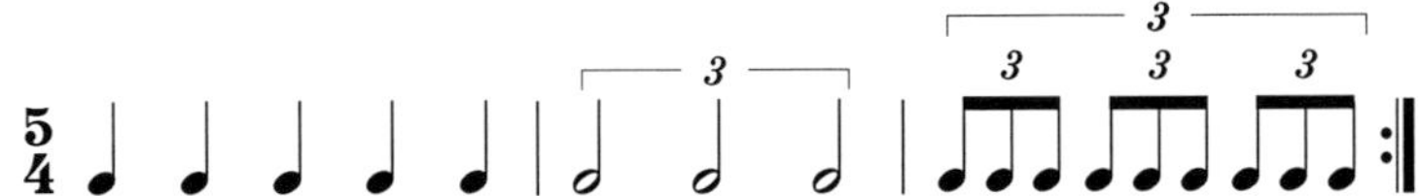

This one may be just as easy for you to do without the step of the triplets, by practicing feeling the large pulse and getting used to going directly from five to nine.

Two over Nine, Four over Nine, Five over Nine, Six over Nine, Seven over Nine, and Eight over Nine

As stated, to accomplish polyrhythms over nine beats, mentally "let go" of the small divisions of the bar, feel the bar as three, and perform the polyrhythms as if they are over three. Perform the polyrhythms using dotted quarters as the beat, instead of quarters.

For example, in 9/8 time, four over nine can look like this:

EXAMPLE 3.68

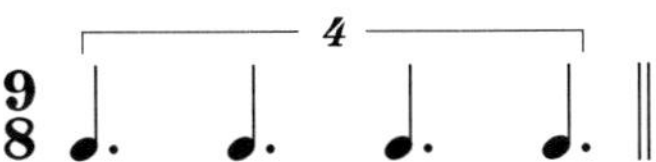

Feel the three dotted quarter beats. Then subdivide each dotted quarter into three dotted 16ths, to create a bar subdivided into 12 bits. As in all the other exercises in this chapter, group these subdivisions into four units of three dotted 16ths each, accomplishing four over three:

EXAMPLE 3.69

So, usually, for two, four, five, or six against nine, you are really performing two, four, five, and six against three.

The same principle applies to 6/8, 12/8, 15/8—all compound times.

Approximating Polyrhythms and Changing Between Many Polyrhythms

When the polyrhythm is too complex, or the tempo is too fast, or the polyrhythms are changing in fast succession, one must approximate. This is not bad, and once you get used to it you can be quite accurate. Too much counting can make the performance stiff. Approximation involves feeling the large pulse, the unit that has the polyrhythm over it, and just "feeling" the subdivision. You can memorize the *feel* of each polyrhythm.

Feeling Polyrhythms Exercise

Set the metronome to a very slow tempo, quarter note = 35–50.

Subdivide each quarter into successively smaller, then larger, subdivisions.

It is helpful and often necessary to imagine the next subdivision before it arrives, in order to perform it correctly. To get used to this, try this exercise with one bar of silence between each beat, and in this beat of silence imagine the next subdivisions:

EXAMPLE 3.70

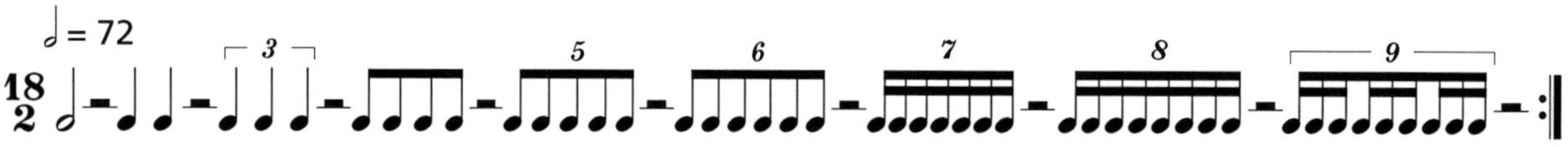

Now get used to it with no rest to imagine and prepare the next subdivision:

EXAMPLE 3.71

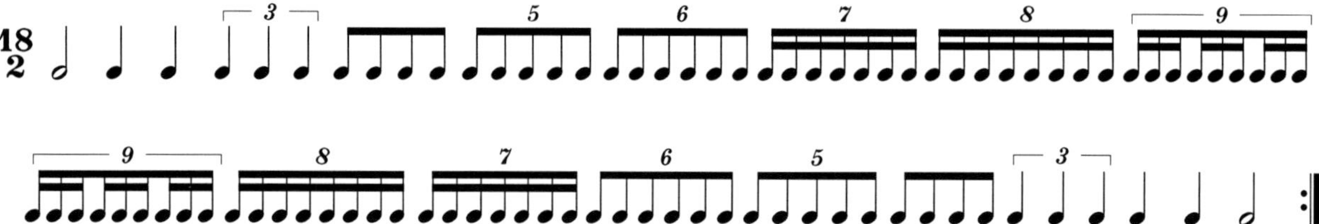

This exercise is good for fluency in all the subdivisions up to nine.

Polyrhythms over Parts of the Bar

The number being "overed" is usually the meter of the piece. However, sometimes the polyrhythm occurs over just part of a bar—over just one beat, over one and a half, or over a bar and a half. There are no rules. That's why I keep saying a polymeter *can* look like so and so. But whatever a polyrhythm is over, the same rules apply. Look at this bar, for example:

EXAMPLE 3.72

This bar has two polyrhythms in it, a three over two and then a four over three. To accomplish the first polyrhythm, you need the lowest common multiple of two and three, which is six. The polyrhythm occurs over the first two quarter notes, so first subdivide these two beats into six, which calls for two triplets. Then group these two triplets into three units of two bits each, and you accomplish the first polyrhythm.

For the second one, you need the lowest common multiple of three and four, which is 12. You take the last three quarter notes of the bar, subdivide them into 16ths, thereby accomplishing the subdivision of 12. Then group the subdivisions into four units of three bits each, and you accomplish the four over three. This is how it looks conceptually:

EXAMPLE 3.73

Look at the excerpt from Elliott Carter's *String Quartet #2* on the following page. You should take the time to analyze, subdivide, and count these out at slow tempos, so that you really know what you're doing. Get used to performing each bar correctly, practicing the bars by themselves, memorizing exactly how they feel, and then put them next to each other. But at performance tempo—since there are so many different subdivisions right after the other and the tempo is fast enough—it is counterproductive to count everything out. You must just feel very strongly the underlying pulse.

Sometimes when the polyrhythms are going by quickly, you can kind of "feel" them in relation to something else. For example, if you have a grouping of five, you can kind of squeeze in an extra beat, or rush the four with an extra note, and accomplish the five. Or you can play a group of six lazily and leave one note out, and accomplish the five. These may be less desirable ways of playing polyrhythms, but sometimes they're more desirable in the real world of performance.

In the excerpt below, at the tempo indicated, it is virtually impossible to do mathematical computation of all the inner subdivision relationships. The polyrhythms must be felt, with swing.

EXAMPLE 3.74 From Elliott Carter's *String Quartet #2:*

Composers sometimes make it very clear how they want polyrhythms phrased, as Carter does here. Also, polyrhythms can come within polyrhythms. Look at Frank Zappa's "The Black Page." He is precise about the phrasing of the polyrhythmic subdivisions:

EXAMPLE 3.75 From Frank Zappa's "The Black Page":

Changing Polyrhythms Exercise

Set the metronome to quarter note = 35–80. Listen to the pulse for a while and sink into it.

First get used to each subdivision. Perform two to each pulse a few times, then three to each pulse, then four, then five, and so on, up to nine, as in exercises 3.70 and 3.71.

Then mix it up. Perform all the relationships of subdivisions of the pulse, going back and forth from one to the other. Also practice leaving a pulse of silence between each subdivision, and imagine the next one before playing it.

In the following, 2/3 means two over three, so you alternate between playing two beats per pulse and three beats per pulse.

2/3 2/5 2/7 2/9

3/4 3/5 3/7 3/8

4/5 4/7 4/9

5/6 5/7 5/8 5/9

6/7 6/8 6/9

7/8 7/9

8/9

Practice each relationship, back and forth, until it feels comfortable.

Then go on to juxtaposing three polyrhythms next to each other, repeating each until internalized:

2/3/4 2/3/5 2/5/6 2/7/9

3/4/5 3/4/7 3/5/6 3/5/7 3/5/8 3/5/9

4/5/6 4/5/7 4/5/8 4/5/9 4/7/8 4/7/9

5/6/7 6/7/8 7/8/9

The possibilities are almost endless.

Now go on to juxtaposing four subdivisions next to each other. This is exactly what you have to do when playing music by Elliott Carter, Charles Wourinen, Frank Zappa, Edgar Varèse, and so many other composers. If you prepare yourself with the exercises outlined in this book, you will feel prepared for complex polymetric challenges encountered in your career.

A Note About Notation: There is some controversy about proper notation of subdivisions in modern music. A professional must learn to sometimes accept unusual or seemingly incorrect notation, extrapolate what is correct from the musical context, and just play it as well as possible.

THE USE OF POLYRHYTHMS IN READING MUSIC

Experience in polyrhythms can make reading accents and syncopations easier.

Any accent can be seen as a solitary event, as a note that sticks out of the texture. Another way to see an accent is as part of a polyrhythm, or as part of a larger rhythmic form. Look for the hemiolas or polyrhythms that are produced by accents. This can make for smoother, more precise performance.

A good example of this can be found in one short spot from Variation XIII in Rachmaninoff's *Rhapsody on a Theme of Paganini* for piano and orchestra:

EXAMPLE 3.76

In the second two measures shown, the orchestra plays a short hemiola of two over three in a cross rhythm to the piano part.

If it's played feeling the accented note in the middle of the bar simply as an accent on the "and of two," the performance of the bar can sound stiff. The rhythmic flow hesitates on that note. However, if the note is felt as part of a hemiola over the whole bar, the rhythmic motion flows through the bar and the performance is smoother and more precise, and loses none of the excitement. It's also easier for the pianist.

Let's look at this in the abstract. Take this common accent in 4/4 time:

EXAMPLE 3.77

This accent comes on the "and" of two, exactly in between the downbeat and beat four. Relating the accent to beat one and beat four creates a hemiola based on two sets of three eighth notes. If you feel this dotted quarter pulse as well as the quarter pulse, the accent just "comes out" of the texture very smoothly and naturally, with no hesitation or jerk on the accented note.

Once you get used to feeling more than one pulse at a time, the accent can take on a whole new character, creating a larger rhythmic phrase. You can feel the hemiola, and switch back to the quarter pulse either on the one of the next bar, or on the two of the next bar, or on the four of the same bar. It opens up phrasing possibilities.

Since you need only two beats to define a pulse, any syncopation can create a new pulse. Take the syncopation on the "and" of three in a bar of 4/4:

EXAMPLE 3.78

That accent implies a new pulse created by that accented note and the downbeat of the following bar. Phrase the accent toward the one of the next bar, creating a nice rhythmic flow with direction. Most syncopations can be analyzed and felt in this way.

Accents and syncopations can go on for a while. Take this violin part in Gershwin's *Porgy and Bess* overture:

EXAMPLE 3.79

The accents in the first bar imply a syncopated three over two (between the "and" of one and three, and then between the "and" of three and the downbeat of the next bar), and then in the second bar he busts out with a six over four, from the "and" of one all the way to the downbeat of the 2/4. He repeats that a couple times, and then, in bar eight, he starts the same pattern on the "and" of one, and stops on the last 16th of beat three. This is the "I Got Rhythm" rhythmic motif. Rhythms are so often "catchy" because of syncopations creating temporary polyrhythm.

Whenever you see a dotted figure, look for the temporary polyrhythm. When the dotted figure is tied to another beat, be on the lookout for more.

EXAMPLE 3.80

You have two hemiolas hidden in example 3.80: (1) an implied four over three, between the downbeat, the fourth 16th of one, and the "and" of two; and (2) a bigger two over three between the downbeat, the "and" of two, and the downbeat of the next bar. Including the fundamental pulse provided by the meter, there are three separate superimposed pulses in that little figure.

If you extend the dotted eighth figure, the four over three pulse emerges:

EXAMPLE 3.81

Seeing the polyrhythms implied by accents and syncopations makes reading music easier and makes rhythmic performance smoother.

SOME NOTES FOR DRUMMERS AND PERCUSSIONISTS

Good rhythm is everybody's responsibility. But due to the nature of percussion and its role in music, rhythmic responsibility falls more on our shoulders than on others'. It's the drummer's or timpanist's job to be a source of rhythmic clarity and strength, so we have to perceive and measure time, to feel rhythm and pulse, quite deeply.

Our instruments have a particularly clear attack, and create relatively short notes, compared to most. Even our longest sustaining instruments, gongs, concert bass drums, and timpani, have an attack with decay. In contrast, winds and strings can sustain a tone without decay, and connect one note to the next. (With rolls we can accomplish this effect, but even rolls consist of successive single strokes.)

Drummers provide the rhythmic skeleton, the support system. It is therefore very important for drummers to consider what comes between the notes, to feel the part of the wave in between the beats, to sense what is occurring in the silences between the sounds, feeling time at all times, especially in the rests. Drummers need to pay particular attention to phrasing and feel.

If we practice with too much focus on being perfectly in time with the metronome, thinking, "This beat, this beat, this beat," we can sound stiff, unmusical. Thinking more like "This goes to this, then to this, then to this," creates a flow, a phrase. This is where feel comes into play: in the phrasing of the music.

So, when practicing the drumset, always think about the big phrase: Where is the beat going?

The following practice routine helps. The idea is to train yourself to always keep the bass line, or some musical line, in the forefront of consciousness while practicing.

This exercise consists of a practice tape of a bass line at many different tempos, to be used as a musical metronome, to instill the awareness of phrase while practicing drum grooves.

Drumset Exercise

First, record the following pattern on a two-track machine:

Record four minutes of a metronome clicking at 40. Stop the tape. Re-set the metronome to quarter note equals 48 and record four minutes of that tempo. Stop the tape, re-set the metronome to 60, and record four minutes of that tempo. Repeat this process a total of 10 times, at quarter note equals 72, 88, 108, 120, 132, 156, 180, and 208. Leave a few seconds between each tempo.

You will have a roughly 44-minute tape of four-minute segments of a click track getting progressively faster.

Next, record a 12-bar blues bass line along with the click in each segment, something like the following:

EXAMPLE 3.82

Now you have a 44-minute tape with both click and a bass line.

Be careful that the bass line stays in as perfect time as possible. I don't recommend a MIDI or a sequenced track, however, because it can feel very monotonous and mechanical. Better if a human being plays it, so it has some character, some feel. It will also be more fun to practice to. Either record the bass yourself (on piano or bass) or get a friend to help you. Best to record the bass line yourself, at least at the slow tempos, to learn the groove from the other side of the coin. Just make sure it lines up well with the click.

If you have a multitrack recording machine, record the eighths as well, along with the click and the bass line. You can play it on snare, or anything clear. It can also be MIDI sequenced.

EXAMPLE 3.83

An advantage to multitracking is that you can change the relative dynamic of the parts, so you can concentrate more on the click one day, the bass another, and the triplets the third.

Practice along with the tape, every day. Keep your pattern very simple—the following drumset jazz pattern is the best:

EXAMPLE 3.84

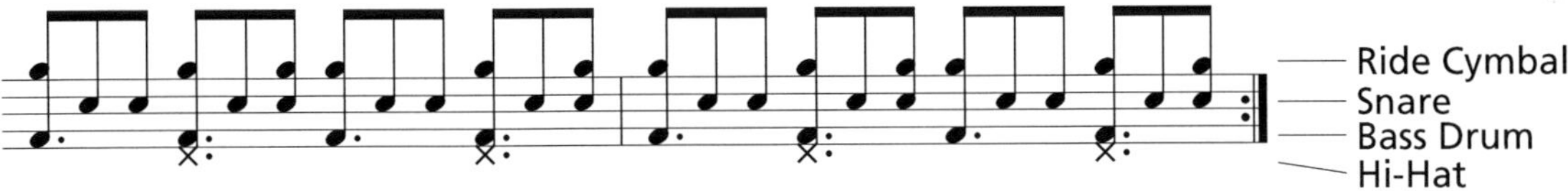

Concentrate on the phrase, and the placement of every note. Make sure each cymbal, hi-hat, and bass drum note falls right in the center of the bass note, precisely with the click, and each limb sounds precisely with the other. Make sure the snare lines up perfectly. Make sure every note you play is *going* to the next downbeat, and going to the really big downbeat, the beginning of the 12-bar phrase. Do something musical to express the phrase, with color or dynamics, without changing the pattern you're playing. No fills.

If you don't keep it simple enough, you will pay attention to the lick you are playing instead of how each note flows with the phrase, how each note contributes to the rhythmic direction. Pay attention to the music, not your own playing. In the slow tempo feel the time between the notes. Fill up the spaces with direction.

Pay attention to your muscles; focus on one at a time, relaxing one after the other. Think about breath, relaxation, focus, and flow, instead of licks or chops.

Keep it simple, doing this exercise every day for at least a month before moving on to any other beats with the tape. Focus on the relative dynamic of each instrument, the clarity of each sound, the exact placement of the sticks. Focus on everything besides the pattern you are playing, so that your playing becomes transparent, so you can focus on everything besides yourself.

This is a great warm-up to do before you move on to everything else that you are practicing that day.

Drummers tend to think about the patterns they are playing more than the music being played. This exercise will help you avoid that tendency.

After you really get the feeling of this exercise, you can begin incorporating some other patterns into the tape practice. Take rhythms from whatever book you are working on and practice them in context of this tape.

You can use any kind of music to create a practice tape like this. Do it with a Latin bass part, lining up your bass drum perfectly with the bass tumbao, while playing the clave on the snare rim, a rumba cymbal part, and hi-hat on two and four. Or do it in rock time, or funk time, or in odd times. As always, use your imagination.

BOOK

4

Rhythm in Performance

Rhythm in Performance

A wide variety of factors affect the quality of rhythmic performance. They range from states of mind and mental attitudes to specific actions and performance practices. Some of these are common knowledge, some rarely discussed. Identifying and considering these issues can help everyone achieve a stronger, more fluid, and deeper rhythmic performance throughout an entire career.

Many of these factors apply not just to rhythm but to musical performance in general. Musicians of all kinds benefit from being aware of them.

Attitude

Attitude is your outlook, the feeling you exude, the manner in which you approach your work. Your attitude affects everything; from one performance to your entire career.

A good rhythmic attitude is confidence without arrogance, an attitude that your inner pulse is right, but with humility that others may be right too. Maintain strength with flexibility. Be ready to adjust rhythmically with the conductor or the musicians around you.

At times you need to hold your ground, to not budge if those around you are rushing or dragging. It takes experience to know when to hold fast or how much to adjust. With a good attitude this will come, without irritating those around you.

This attitude applies to pitch as well. Some players are sure they have the "right" pitch, and won't budge. This can lead to out-of-tune performances and an unpleasant atmosphere.

Good attitude leads to good performance. Be a team player. Support others rhythmically.

Relaxation

Relax. Relaxation leads to good rhythmic performance. It opens your senses, opens your ears to what is going on around you, allows you to feel and express pulse easily. Relaxation allows you to play what you've been practicing, without thinking about it.

If you are too relaxed, there's nothing there. Relaxation doesn't mean lack of energy and concentration. The best performance state is relaxed, calmly focused high energy.

Stay relaxed during practice sessions. Take breaks. Rub your arms; stretch. Keep your muscles loose.

Avoid practicing too hard; avoid pushing. If you push your practice, your performance will be pushed, too. Pushed muscles get hurt. You can't pull grass up to make it grow faster; it has to grow at its own rate. Make sure to water it just right, give it lots of sunshine and good nutrition, and it will grow as fast as it can. Be committed, pay attention, work hard, stay relaxed.

For feedback on your relaxation state play Metronome Exercise 10, the displaced pulse unison:

EXERCISE 4.1

Pick a relaxing tempo, perhaps mm=60–90. Breathe slowly. Relax all the muscles in your body, moving from top to bottom—head, neck, shoulders, arms, torso, stomach, pelvis, legs, and feet—while doing the exercise. Then move the metronome up, to 120, 160, 190, 240, but only as fast as you can stay relaxed, focusing on muscle relaxation, not the tempo.

Time away from music helps your music making. Take time off; take vacations from music now and then. Work on your physical state. Yoga, meditation, and exercising help with general relaxation. Eat well. Too much coffee disturbs relaxation.

Remember that growth occurs when you are at rest, so practice hard but take the time to rest all you need.

Nerves

Nerves affect almost everyone's rhythmic performance. It's easy but not necessarily realistic to say "Don't get nervous." Understanding your nerves, and dealing with them, is as valuable as fending them off.

Nerves have a good side. They sharpen acuity and can help rhythmic performance. The trick is to accept them, learn about your reactions to them, and positively channel the nervous energy.

Study your reactions to nerves and stress. Analyze the effect they have on your performance. Pay attention to what happens to you rhythmically when you get nervous. You may rush from excitement, or drag from caution. Whatever nerves do to you, you can compensate for it.

One way to neutralize nerves is to focus on your inner pulse. While waiting to play, when you feel nervousness coming on, start pulsing. Do the chest pulse; breathe in time. Feel the pulse and focus on the music. Your nerves will subside, and you can channel that energy into your performance.

One experience in particular taught me about my reactions to nerves. As a student at Tanglewood one summer, I was assigned the snare drum part in the *1812 Overture* in a performance with the Boston Symphony Orchestra, Seiji Ozawa conducting. A quiet snare solo ushers in the famous melody. Approaching this solo in rehearsal; I noticed that my hands were sweaty and both they and my knees were shaking. At that point in my life, in the context of where and with whom I was playing, I felt like *my whole life* depended on playing that part. What pressure I put on myself.

I started the solo. Maestro Ozawa stopped the orchestra and said, "Snare drum, you must play this part as if your life depended on it."

As if I wasn't already doing that! That's when I really got nervous. My eyes glossed over, my knees wobbled, and I couldn't see or remember the part. It was all I could do to stand up and watch the conductor. So I just pulsed as hard as I could, and made up a snare solo. He smiled; he seemed to like it.

Nervousness happens. If all else fails, pulse.

You can't reproduce what goes on in real life in a practice room, so sometimes sneak in a recorder and record yourself in rehearsals or performances, even at auditions. Play plenty of mock auditions, and record yourself. Perform for your friends and colleagues. Colleagues are the hardest to play for; they can make you more nervous than anyone, but that's good. The experience will help you at auditions.

Try running up and down some stairs, and then playing. Being out of breath and having an accelerated heartbeat simulate nervousness. The more you can practice being nervous, the more you can deal with it when it happens in real life. If you can learn to relax and deal with nervousness, you can channel it into an exciting high-energy performance.

Sight-reading also helps. Pay close attention to what happens when you get to hard sections, and what happens during easy sections. Sight-read with friends. Record yourself sight-reading. Sight-read in public. Make yourself nervous.

Concentration

Concentrate. Focus. Without concentration, pulse fluctuates. Even the most experienced players keep a continuous, conscious focus on the pulse. For a good performance, you can't be lackadaisical. Good rhythm doesn't "just happen," even if you have the best sense of time on the planet. You have to really concentrate every moment.

It's possible to over-concentrate. Your attention becomes so focused on your part that you lose touch with what is going on around you. It's like tunnel vision. If you try too hard, you "push," and the tempo can rush. You tire more quickly. Therefore, try to keep an open, relaxed calmness to your concentration.

Thoughts and emotions can interfere with your concentration. The best thing to do when you find this happening is to be aware of them, and just let them go, returning to the rhythm at hand. If this is happening while you are practicing, take a break. Five minutes of concentrated practice is better than an hour of distracted mechanics.

Emotional states affect concentration. If you are "charged" emotionally, it's harder to concentrate. At the same time, some people are able to harness their emotions, and can concentrate better when, say, they're angry. Learn what emotional states trigger good concentration, and use that knowledge.

Meditation is a great way to "let go" of distracting thoughts and emotions. This is the purpose and practice of meditation. A daily meditation routine also helps you maintain that calm, energetic, focused state, the best for performance. Take 20 minutes to disengage from thoughts and emotions every day. Sit comfortably and follow your breathing. As thoughts come up, just let them go. Return to your breathing as the thoughts drift off. Breathe in and out and in and out; let that be all there is for a little while.

Practice through distractions. Concentrate while the neighbor's radio is on, or while a conversation is buzzing, or near a construction site. Develop the ability to focus on your work no matter what is going on.

Counting

Counting helps develop your pulse, rhythm, and meter. Count out loud sometimes when practicing. If you find you can't count out loud while practicing a particular passage, it means you're not feeling the underlying meter; it means technique is becoming more important than music. Counting can help assimilate all aspects of rhythm. Counting the bars and the longer phrases helps keep the larger architecture in mind, which helps performance.

Counting out loud is pretty hard to do if you play a wind instrument. Wind players should work on counting when away from their instrument, when playing piano, practicing their parts on piano, or doing metronome exercises.

Counting bars is important, especially for brass and percussion players, with those long rests. Be expert at it.

Count strongly while practicing rhythms that you are working on for performance, auditioning, or musicianship class.

Some people are embarrassed to count out loud, feeling that counting out loud is a form of weakness, that it implies that you don't have good rhythm. That's not true at all. The stronger you can count, the stronger your rhythm. Just don't do it all the time, and not during performance.

Count one bar in your mind before you perform a piece, for rhythmic security and to feel the meter. It settles the tempo, helps you avoid taking too fast a tempo, and calms the nerves. It's especially important at auditions to count silently before you play.

Practice counting as if it is part of the piece you are playing. Record the count before you record a passage and check later to see if the counted tempo and your performance tempo match. You may be surprised at how different they are. Count with rhythmic clarity. Learn to count with such confidence that those around you will feel secure about the tempo.

Count while sight-reading. It helps maintain an even pulse, and helps keep odd times without slipping. If you can't count through it, you can't really play it.

The way you count can affect the character of the piece you perform. Try counting in different ways, emphasizing the one, then the two, then the three, then the four. Record yourself counting with different personalities, different feels, different kinds of energy. Find the right kind of count for the piece you are performing. A German count is different from a French count, the syntax of the language is distinct, and French music is just different than German. Count in different languages. Count a march or count a tango. Count staccato, count legato, count impressionistic, or count heroic. Count with character.

Clarity

The clearer your rhythm, the better your performance. The more clarity you have about exactly how you want each note, phrase, and dynamic, the better.

Rhythmic clarity is achieved by thinking about and expressing the following:

- Pulse
- Meter
- The articulation of each note
- The shape of the body of the note
- The length of each note
- The end of each note
- The exact distance between notes
- The fullness of the rests

- Rhythmic "placing"—early, late, right on
- The exact dynamics of each note and phrase
- The rhythmic shape of the phrase

In other words, think about everything. No fuzzy edges, no uncertainty about length, rests, dynamics, shape, or anything. Have an idea about how you want every little thing.

Always feel the inner pulse with clarity. Express the meter of the piece. Keep the metric feeling alive all the time. Be clear about time.

Think about each phrase. Try it a few different ways, and then be decisive about your choices.

Slow practice is great for developing clarity, as practicing slowly gives you the time to really think about each note.

It's like public speaking. If you are uncertain about what you want to say, or which words you want to say it with, less is expressed. Clarity in preparation leads to clarity in performance.

Clarity Exercise

Play four bars of quarter notes. Keep the pulse and attack of each note precisely exact, just change the length of each note, as follows:

EXAMPLE 4.2

The dots and lines above the notes express the relative lengths of the notes. The first note is quite staccato, then each note is progressively longer. The downbeat of the third bar is the longest. Then make each note progressively shorter until you get back to the downbeat of bar one, the staccato note. Repeat, paying close attention to both the length of each note and the length of the rests between the notes.

Keep the pulse strong and clear; the attack remains strictly in time.

Do the same exercise in reverse, the long note at the beginning and the staccato notes in the middle.

The simplicity of the exercise allows you to concentrate both on the clarity of pulse and the shape and length of each note.

It is important to pay attention and get feedback regarding the clarity of your physical movements, especially for conductors. Clear communication counting off, motions bringing in other players, and eye contact enhance the vitality and expressiveness of the performance.

Don't be afraid to write clear notes or instructions to yourself in your music. It's not a weakness. Write legibly, so if you come back to perform the same piece a year later, you will know with no uncertainty exactly what you meant.

Feel

Music and rhythm are all about feel. You can line up exactly with the metronome, but if it doesn't feel good, well, then, it just doesn't. If you are playing mechanically, like a metronome, you can have a great pulse but no feel at all.

Feel is a term used to describe rhythmic performance. Drummers are described by their feel. A good drummer just feels good—"has a good feel." How do you develop a good feel? How do you make it swing and groove?

It's mostly about pulse. Pulse is a feeling, and a good pulse just feels good. It is rare that what is expressed will not feel good if the performer is feeling the inner pulse. But a strong pulse isn't enough.

Express the meter—that helps with feel. Be clear about feeling the downbeat. Phrase to and away from the downbeat, or to and away from whatever note you choose, but phrase, always phrase in some manner. Dynamics make for feel. Relaxation makes for good feel. Roundness, too; avoid edginess.

Feel the harmony, and move with it. How do you rhythmically play a dominant-tonic cadence or any modulation? Don't just play through it; do something dynamically and rhythmically with it, perhaps pulling back and lightening up. "Feel" it, and do what your feeling dictates.

Record yourself and listen back. Can you move to it easily, clap with it, dance to it? It can be in good time, but if you can't move easily to it, there is something missing in the feel.

How you play in ensemble creates the feel. If you have a good attitude, if you keep an open mind and ear, if you rhythmically support the musicians around you, you will generate good feel.

Feeling implies emotion. Rhythm, music in general, is all about expressing emotion. Pulse is a feeling, and the more feeling you have about it, the deeper you feel it, the more it will generate emotion, the more "feel" it will have. You have to *want* it. Pulse has to be important to you, and if you want it, you will express it with feeling. Desire is a feeling. If you really desire a good performance, that feeling will come through. If you care about those playing around you, that feeling will come through. If you understand and empathize with the thoughts and emotions being expressed by the composer, that emotion will come through. In short, feel is one's humanity expressed through pulse and rhythm.

If you study hard, have desire, feel the pulse strongly, and care about the musicians around you, feel happens.

Fluidity and Flexibility

Rhythmic fluidity and flexibility are essential for strong musical rhythmic performance. Without flexibility, rhythm is stiff, unmusical. Consider the parable of the two trees, one stiff and proud, the other strong but supple. When the hurricane came through, the stiff one broke in two, while the supple one gave to, bent, and survived. Rhythmically, be strong and supple.

Being supple means having your ears open, ready to adjust the tempo, pitch, or color. Practice your pieces at many different tempos. Be ready for surprises. Stay relaxed and concentrated on the music at hand, avoiding tension, staying loose. Fluidity means being sensitive to others, allowing a push or a pull easily, within limits. Rhythm flows, like water; it's never stiff.

Flexibility also means being able to do more than one thing at a time. If you can keep your mind supple, you can keep a pulse, count bars, and pass your colleague a pencil. Discussing a musical point while counting bars takes an open, supple, flexible attitude.

Flexibility Exercise 1

Find a colleague who wants to work on this with you. Play a pulse unison: Metronome Exercise 9.

EXAMPLE 4.3

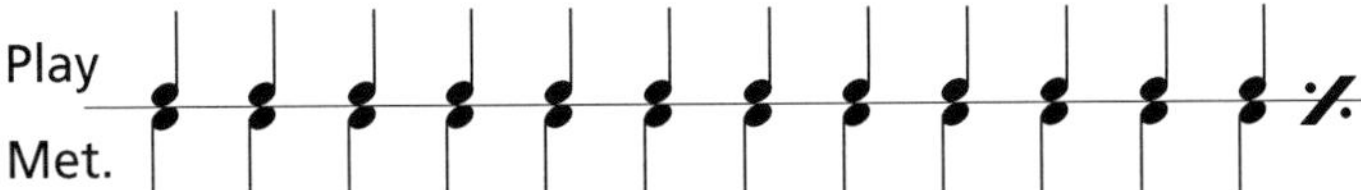

Player one is the leader, the metronome. Player one gently changes the pulse, slower or faster. Player two plays along, maintaining as smooth a pulse unison as possible, while the leader goes slower and faster. Take turns being the leader.

Flexibility Exercise 2

Use the same process, except play a displaced pulse unison: Metronome Exercise 10.

EXAMPLE 4.4

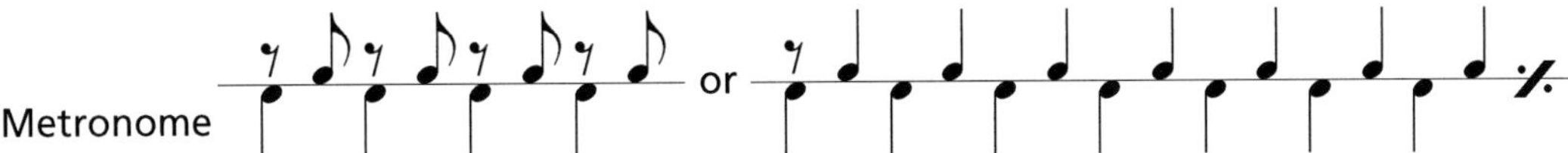

The leader is the metronome and can gently speed up or slow down.

You can perform this exercise with a recording device instead of a second player. Record yourself playing a pulse that is speeding up and slowing down. Then play a pulse unison, or a displaced pulse unison, along with the recording.

Find a metronome with which you can change the pulse without turning it off. Record a metronome pulse that is gently speeding up and slowing down, creating a click track that doesn't keep steady time. Play along with it.

While doing these exercises pay attention to your muscles; stay loose and relaxed. It's hard to be flexible if you're holding tension.

Other ways to practice flexibility: Practice in a position to which you're unaccustomed. Change the position of your body or the music stand. Put your leg up on the chair, move in new ways, find strange positions (perhaps on your back). Use instruments that you're uncomfortable with. Practice in strange places, perhaps with distractions. Play foreign, strange, or uncomfortable instruments. Try talking while practicing.

Use the recordings of shifting pulse you made to practice flexibility. Besides playing pulse unison or displaced pulse unison, play the metronome exercises with subdivisions, and play them over a subtly shifting pulse.

Rubato

Rubato is related to flexibility. In the strict sense, it means to be able to stretch time without losing touch with the underlying pulse.

Rubato Exercise 1

Play a pulse unison with a metronome at about mm=48–60. As you are doing so, start to push your notes slightly ahead of the metronome till you can hear the metronome pulses clicking after your own. Gently pull forward, and then pull back together with the metronome, as follows:

EXAMPLE 4.5

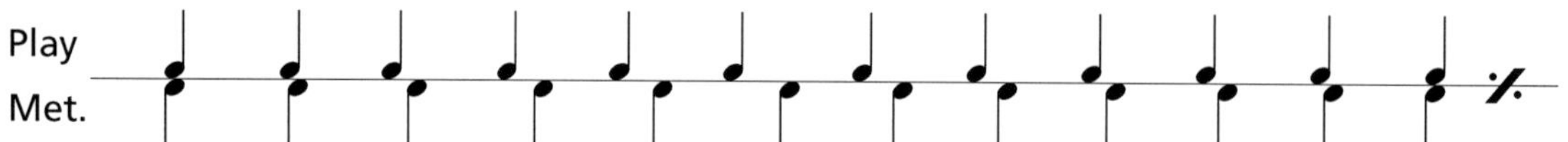

Be aware of the space between the metronome clicks and your own clicks. Get that space as long as you can, and then pull back rhythmically, gently closing the gap until you pull again into pulse unison.

Rubato Exercise 2

Try pulling rhythmically *behind* the pulse, and then push back again, as follows:

EXAMPLE 4.6

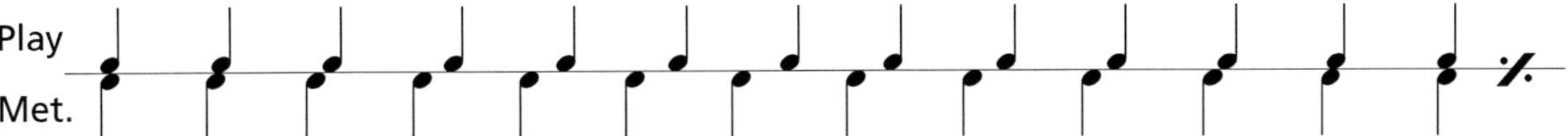

Try both of these exercises at different tempos. Challenge yourself to pull as far away as you can from the metronome pulse and then back again.

Accelerandos and Ritardandos

Accelerandos and ritardandos are easier to accomplish smoothly if you keep the smaller subdivisions in mind. Your tempo changes will sound logical if you can mentally keep track of the subdivisions while changing tempo.

Have a target tempo and practice accelerating to it, or pulling back to it. Let's say you pick mm=100 as your target tempo. Listen to the metronome and memorize the tempo. Turn off the metronome. Record yourself playing a slower pulse, then accelerate till you feel you have reached the target tempo of 100. Keep recording for a bit. Listen back, note how the accelerando felt, and check whether you settled into the target tempo.

Playing Ahead of and Behind the Beat

Being able to play ahead of or behind the beat is an important skill. It can help you maintain the tempo when those around you are rushing or dragging, and is necessary for successful ritardandos and accelerandos.

Here's an exercise: Set the metronome to a moderate tempo, mm=52–80. Play a displaced pulse unison just ahead of or behind the beat, as follows:

EXAMPLE 4.7

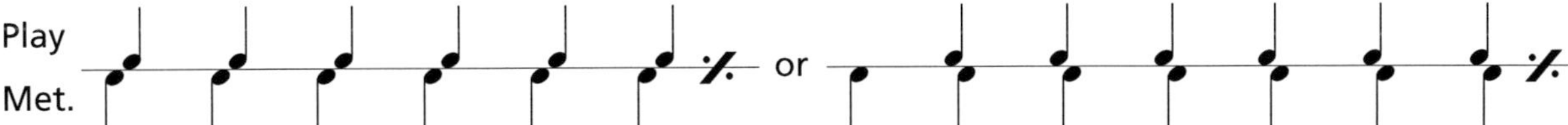

Be sensitive to how far behind the beat you are, and hold it right there. See how closely you can anticipate the beat. Challenge yourself with different tempos and beat placements. It's not easy to consistently play just after the beat.

Dealing with Rushing and Dragging

Rushing means getting faster, and dragging means getting slower, in relation to the desired tempo. The term also can mean simply playing too fast or too slow.

Rushing and dragging can also mean consistently playing ahead of or behind the beat when you don't realize it. Everyone does it to some extent. As is true with pitch, nobody's perfect, but you want to avoid it as much as possible.

The first step to avoiding rushing or dragging is to become sensitive to it. Listen for it at performances and at concerts. Become aware of it in your own playing when listening back to yourself. Try doing it on purpose; see how it feels. Record it and listen back to it.

Performing the rubato exercises, the ahead-of- and behind-the-beat exercises, and all of the metronome exercises will also help. If you don't concentrate on becoming sensitive to rushing or dragging, you will do it as soon as you turn off the metronome.

Rushing and dragging can be the result not only of poor concentration but also of nerves, tension, or anxiety. It can also be the result of not internalizing the pulse enough.

Desire and Motivation

The most important key to good rhythmic performance is desire. Desire motivates accomplishment. If you want good rhythm, and you are honest with yourself, you will put in the time and attention to develop it, both in study and in the moment of performance.

There is long-term desire and short-term desire. Long-term desire motivates you to get up early to study, and to keep at it for years. Short-term desire is wanting it *now*, which is necessary for good performance. Without immediate motivation, your performance can lack the necessary fire. Without the desire your performance will be flat, no matter how good your intrinsic sense of rhythm.

Long-term desire will ebb and flow. Don't worry if you have a phase in which you just don't feel like it. Let that period be one in which you are internalizing what you have been working on. And then, when you feel the motivation again, take advantage of it; get up early and work hard. Don't put it off.

Desire is an emotion, emotion creates feeling, and feeling is what rhythm is all about. The more you desire, the more feeling your performance will provide, and feeling is what people want from music.

Honesty

Be honest about your performance. There is always room for improvement. Some people think their rhythm is pretty good, when it actually has major faults. Pay critical attention and always be open to suggestions and improvement.

At the same time, if you over-criticize yourself, lighten up. Some say their rhythm is terrible, when it's actually pretty good. It's all relative, just keep getting better.

Faking It

Faking it is an important part of good musicianship. Everyone makes mistakes. No one concentrates perfectly all the time; everybody gets lost once in a while. Also, things happen. The pages stick together, or the wind blows your music off the stand. Lights go out, things drop, doors open—you name it.

When things happen, faking it is essential. Faking means: when lost, play *something,* with strong rhythm, ideally in the same key and style as what you were performing. This allows the conductor or your colleagues to continue without a problem. They will thank you for it. The show must go on.

One can prepare for these moments. Being prepared is an attitude. Practice playing with strong rhythm when you are unsure of what you are doing. Sight-reading is excellent for this, by yourself or with others. Somehow, learn to continue when you get lost. Don't stop...don't stop...keep going until you find your place. Improvise. (If improvisation isn't yet among your skills, study it.) Work on flexibility. Put yourself in situations that are beyond your capabilities, and contribute rhythmically.

Faking it is not the ideal solution. To avoid having to fake it, prepare as best you can, try not to get lost, and keep as high a standard of performance as possible. But when all else fails, come through with something. Some of the most exciting performances occur when the conductor loses place for a moment. Some of the best performers in the world have occasionally been the best fakers, perhaps precisely because of that. Just think of it as a short improvisation. The energy rush can be exhilarating.

This advice comes from an expert faker. I started out as a trombone player, and trombone music is written in the bass and tenor clef. I had no piano training, so when I picked up the drums, I could not read the treble clef. Jobs came quickly, and they sometimes included xylophone, bell, or vibes parts, all written in the treble clef. Sometimes I would come to a job and just not be able to read the notes, so I would have to just sight-read the part rhythmically as strongly as possible, then go home and memorize the notes by rote for the next rehearsal. I got some very funny looks from bandleaders, but somehow survived, slowly gaining experience in the treble clef. I don't recommend taking this approach unless it's absolutely necessary.

Character

Character refers to the personality, flavor, tradition, and spirit expressed in the performance of music. Character brings music to life, makes it human, gives it meaning. Character also determines how you interpret a rhythmic figure.

The words *character* and *personality* are almost interchangeable here.

The deeper one's knowledge, and the greater one's imagination, the more character one can give to a musical figure or to an entire piece. Consider the following methods for determining the character of a piece:

- Study the performance traditions for that piece.
- Learn about the language, life, and culture of the composer, especially around the time of the piece's composition.
- Become familiar with the culture the piece is describing. If you are in a Mendelssohn phase, for example, look at photos of the Hebrides to conduct the *Hebrides* overture. Listen to tarantellas and other Italian music before a performance of the *Italian* symphony, and read the chapter in a history book about the Reformation for conducting or playing that symphony. Explore the spiritual intent or meaning behind a composition.
- Envision the scene or personality the piece is describing or expressing.
- Imagine your own meaning, intent, picture, or scene for the piece.
- Try to express the emotional intent or content in every musical moment. Is it romantic, heroic, erotic, stoic, intellectual, infantile, excited, bored, joyous, sad, searching, or something else?

This is why it's so important to study more than just the piece that you're working on. Study other music of the world; study language, cultures, and biographies, and study past performance traditions.

All these considerations can affect how you play any rhythmic figure. By shaping a rhythm, you can change its sound, mood, and meaning. And every rhythm has infinite possibilities of interpretation.

Take the dotted eighth–16th, a ubiquitous rhythmic figure used by virtually every composer in the history of Western concert music:

EXAMPLE 4.8

This rhythmic figure can differ depending on the composer, performer, the piece, or even the part of the piece. It can sound like Beethoven, Bach, Mozart, or Mahler, and it is up to the performer to play it in such a way that it *does* sound like either Beethoven, Bach, Mozart, or Mahler.

You can analyze the subtle rhythmic differences till your face turns blue. The three notes can be the same dynamically, or the first can be a bit louder than the second, or the second louder than the first but a bit less than the third, or the third the loudest. You can crescendo through the three, or diminuendo. You can attack each note differently, the first with a *da* sound, the second with a hard *ka,* and the third with a *boom* or a *ta,* or any combination of articulations.

The lengths and shapes of each note can vary in myriad different ways, with the first note played legato with a swell, the second a sharp staccato, and the third legato but with a quick diminuendo. The space between the notes can vary, and the rhythm itself can vary, making the 16th early or quite late, and fat or skinny. In short, there are infinite possibilities for playing this figure.

The performer can make these decisions analytically and intellectually, but they can be quite hard to articulate. With experience they are made intuitively, emotionally, and sound right if one has studied well. The point is that rhythmic nuance is how musicians express emotion, personality—character.

The best lesson I ever received on character was at a student orchestra rehearsal directed by Leonard Bernstein. He stopped abruptly in the middle of the "March of the Toreadors" from Bizet's *Carmen* and said impatiently, "Does anybody know what this piece is about?" There was a long pause, until one brave soul timidly said what we were all thinking, "It's about the bullfighters walking into the bull ring." Bernstein bellowed, "Of course it's about the toreadors marching into the bull ring, but it's so much more. It's the crowds cheering, the flags waving, the dust, the noise, the atmosphere charged in anticipation of a battle to the death, the tight black pants and flowing red shirts of the toreadors, the brightly colored free-flowing dresses of the señoras, the looks of anticipation on all their faces, the lancers, the horses, the pride, the entire history of Castillian culture culminating in this very bullfight. Now let's try it again."

We played it again. The notes were the same, but the rhythm was transformed, with a heightened spirit and clarity of expression. Even though most of us had never been to a bullfight, or even to Spain for that matter, we all suddenly felt as if we knew exactly how to play the piece. Bernstein had become a proud old bullfighter, transmitting the spirit of the moment through his gestures, motions, and expressions. Without saying a word about how to place or play this note or that note, he got the entire orchestra to play rhythmically, to paint a picture, to express the personality and meaning of the piece. He brought out the piece's *character.*

Music from Around the World

There are so many reasons it's important to study music from all over the world, especially in this day and age.

To understand the character of the many pieces you may have occasion to play, a broad knowledge of musical styles, conventions, and history around the globe is invaluable. To play Mendelssohn's *Italian* symphony, it helps to be able to play a tarantella. To well perform the music of Carlos Chavez, Manuel De Falla, Silvestre Revueltas, and other Latin American composers, an understanding of and facility in Latin American music helps to make their music come alive. Debussy was inspired by Indonesian music, so an awareness of Indonesian music helps bring out the color of the gamelan in some of his pieces. A familiarity with Hungarian traditions deepens the rhythmic performance of Béla Bartók.

This principle is just as applicable, if not more so, to contemporary compositions. The more you know about the background and history of the compositions you play, the more character and rhythm you can bring to your performances. The more you play jazz, the easier you'll play and the more depth you'll bring to the music of George Gershwin, Leonard Bernstein, Duke Ellington, Maurice Ravel, Darius Milhaud, and Igor Stravinsky. If you have spent time playing Indonesian music, those pieces by composers influenced by Indonesian music—Lou Harrison, Colin McPhee, and to some extent Benjamin Britten—will make more sense and have more depth. Knowing rock music gives power to the music of John Adams, John Corigliano, and Frank Zappa. The San Francisco Symphony has performed with Metallica and the Grateful Dead, and the Chicago Symphony recorded a special for MTV with Smashing Pumpkins. More and more string ensembles are performing arrangements of rock and jazz tunes, and are accompanying pop groups. In a very tangible way, the more you know about more genres of music, the broader your professional opportunities.

Even without a direct correlation to any particular composer or composition, studying other forms of music can add levels of expression to performance, simply by broadening one's musical vocabulary. The wider your base of knowledge, and the deeper your cultural roots, the broader your range of expression can expand.

Especially relevant to the theme of this book, studying the music from all around the world can contribute to and improve your sense of pulse and rhythm. Studying and playing African music deepens your sense of groove, and opens worlds of polyrhythm not found anywhere else. Studying and performing Indonesian gamelan helps with rhythmic memory, and settles you into an entirely different kind of groove. Playing Latin music helps with syncopation. Facility with Mexican and flamenco makes shifting from 3/4 to 6/8 easy.

In short, open yourself up to as much music as possible. It will improve your rhythm, and develop your musical character.

Here are some specific suggestions for relating various types of world music to specific compositions:

Listen to Japanese vocal music, and then listen to Giacomo Puccini's *Madame Butterfly.*

Listen to a Balinese gamelan, and then listen to Benjamin Britten's *Prince of the Pagodas.*

Listen to Mexican huapango music, and then listen to "America" from *West Side Story.*

Listen to some flamenco, and then listen to the last movement from *Estancia* by Alberto Ginastera.

Listen to *Schelomo* by Ernest Bloch, and then get into klezmer music. Feel the similarity of rhythmic and harmonic cadence in so many klezmer performances and many of Mahler's compositions.

Language

Facility with foreign languages can help deepen rhythmic performance, and enhance sensitivity to the character of various musical styles and compositions. Understanding French gives another level of depth and color to the performance of French music. Speaking Spanish helps one feel the rhythms of Latin music. Speaking German brings power to the performance of lieder and German choral music. Chinese deepens your appreciation for pitch-bending nuance.

So study foreign language. Take courses in a few and pick one to study in depth. Listen to foreign radio stations to appreciate the rhythm of speech, the flow of the words, the uses of pitch and articulation. Hear it as music; make up nonsense syllables that approximate it. Let it inspire you.

Music and language evolved together. The language of a culture is a root source for the rhythm of a culture's music. That's why language is so important for appreciating a culture's musical character.

All Art Forms

All the different branches of art evolved concurrently. Knowledge of the history of art in general deepens your appreciation of music.

Visit museums. Study art. Appreciate rhythm frozen in time. Art can express motion when there is no motion. Appreciate Rodin's sculpture for form, balance, inner strength, and integrity. Allow art to inspire your rhythmic performance. Be inspired by how the masters of the old Dutch school, Rembrandt and Vermeer, use light. Then use light as an element in your playing. Contemporary visual artists, too, can inspire your performance of contemporary music—with energy and chaos. It is said the human eye can discern about three million different shades of color, so allow three million different colors of tone and rhythm into your performance. Art leads to new ways of thinking about music.

Working with a Conductor

When performing in an orchestra, you need to pay attention to many aspects of rhythm and musical inflection: your own inner pulse, the rhythm and phrasing you personally want to achieve, the rhythm of the musicians right next to you, the rhythm of your orchestral section, and the rhythm of the band or orchestra as a whole. Then, as well as rhythm, there's pitch, nuance, character, tone, and dynamics. On top of all this, one has to consistently pay attention to, respond to, and make music with and through the conductor. If you play in an orchestra, learning how to work with a conductor is as important as any aspect of learning to play your instrument.

The trick is to learn how to play confidently no matter what's going on, and there's a lot to learn to be able to do so.

Every conductor is different. Some provide a clear pulse, others not so clear. Some go fast in general, others lay back and move slowly. Some beat large, some beat small. Some beat in jagged angular motions, and expect you to react precisely to their beat. Others are fluid, and expect you to "breathe" with their motions. Some express through their fingers, others the wrist, others the arms—with others the whole body can become involved. And with some conductors you have a hard time predicting.

Every conductor has his or her own likes and dislikes, a preferred approach to music making, balance, and orchestration. Some like to bring out percussion, others wish the composers had left percussion out of their pieces entirely. Some like lots of sound, others are more careful with volume. Some like blends of sound, others like to hear each instrument as a solo voice. The better you are at reading the conductor, and the quicker you figure out his or her style, the more success you will have.

The conductor imagines and provides the pulse, but you perform it, so take his pulse and make it your own. This is easier done with some conductors than with others. A good conductor is very clear in providing the pulse, but even with the best conductors, there can be many ways to interpret the pulse provided. The stronger your own inner pulse, the better you'll be able to perform his pulse. If your own pulse is not strong, the conductor won't feel confidence in your performance, even if you are reading him well. This takes practice and quick reflexes, because you generally have only two beats to start the piece (it takes only two beats to define a pulse.) Often the conductor only gives you one, the upbeat, and you have to come in confidently.

Pay close attention to the conductor *before* she starts conducting. Consciously or not, body language often communicates the rhythm before indicating the upbeat. Also, the conductor likes to see you paying attention. Have your eyes up even if you don't play the first note.

Orchestras also have personalities of their own—how much breath they take before coming in, who leads, who rushes and drags. As an orchestral musician you need to strike a balance between fitting into the orchestra and following the conductor.

There's always a balance between what the conductor is doing and what the orchestra is performing. No individual can know exactly what the conductor is thinking all the time, and no conductor can make a performer do anything exactly as desired. There is always a gap between the conductor's motions and the performance of the group. The actual performance is a consensus between individuals and the group.

Take the downbeat, for example. When the conductor begins the piece, how do you know exactly when to come in? Conductors may expect you to play exactly at the bottom of their stroke, but that rarely happens. How do you know exactly where the bottom of the stroke is? At belt level? Belly button level? Chest level? And the level can change depending on the tempo or dynamic or technique. The orchestra plays somewhere after the bottom of the stroke, as the baton is traveling up.

The ictus of the conductor's beating pattern is the point where the conductor's beat changes direction. In 4/4 time, there are four ictuses:

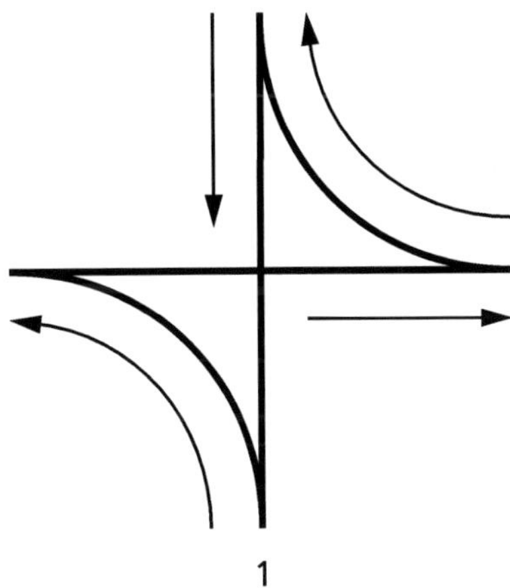

In 3/4 time, there are three:

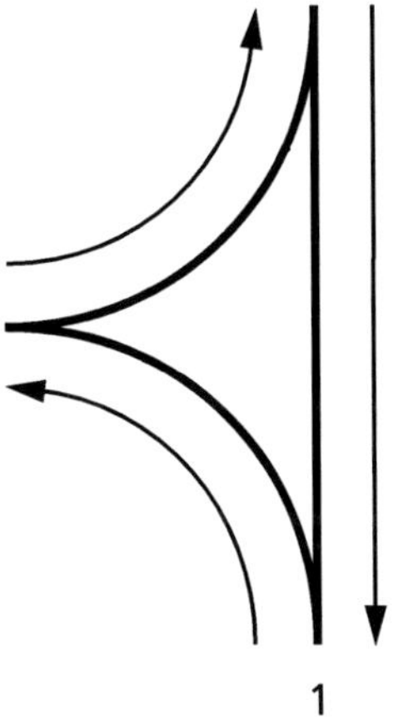

The *downbeat* is always the one of the bar.

The point in time after the ictus when it is the right time to play depends on the style of the conductor, the tradition of the orchestra, the tempo of the piece, the style of the piece, and where you are in the piece. Any orchestra member that performs precisely when the stick comes down soon learns that he is coming in early.

The delay at the beginning of the piece, the first downbeat, is in general much more than the delay once the piece gets going. The slower the piece, the more time between the ictus and the sound. The faster the piece, the closer the musicians play with the conductor's motions, especially once things get going. In general, the larger the orchestra, the longer it takes to get going.

It's easier to adjust time by moving forward a bit than pulling back a bit. The same with pitch: it generally feels easier to tune up into a pitch than to tune down. We are more sensitive to flatness than to sharpness, in general. Just so with pulse: it's easier to adjust slightly faster than to pull the tempo back. Therefore, be particularly careful not to take the conductor's tempo too fast, as you'll then have the difficult job of pulling back.

Once the piece gets going, be vigilant about not rushing. It is a human tendency to get faster.

What do you do when the conductor makes a mistake? In a sense, you can't depend on the conductor. If she loses her place, you must still come in correctly. If the conductor gives you a cue that you *know* is wrong, do not come in. You'd better be absolutely sure, though. If the conductor is lost, she may need help from the orchestra. Know your part well enough that if the conductor gets lost, you don't. At the same time, if everybody is lost, the conductor has to save it, and you go with her.

The orchestra can have a mind of its own. The individual performer must balance between the reality of the performance and the wishes of the conductor. If the orchestra starts rushing or dragging, pushing or pulling, and the conductor is making faces and conducting slower or faster than the sound you are hearing, do you go with the band, or go with the conductor? While you can try to help the conductor, you must go with the band. No matter how right you are with the conductor, if you come in early or late or in a different tempo than the band, *you* are out of time. If the conductor is wrong and you follow him, *you* make the mistake that everyone hears. Remember: *la batuta no suene*—the baton makes no sound.

Mathematics

There are so many relationships between music and math that it's no mystery students of one often have a proclivity for the other.

The word *arithmetic,* for example, has its roots in *art* and *measure,* two very musical terms. The art of measurement and the grouping of numbers are both musical and mathematical concerns; mathematicians perceive and measure things, and musicians perceive and measure time. Even the word *arithmetic* has rhythm in it, just spelled a little differently.

Arithmetic is used to read rhythm. Starting with a whole note, a unity of one big beat, we divide it into two halves, and four quarter notes. These notes are divided into eighth, 16th, 32nd, and shorter notes. In 12/8 time, we divide each measure into 12 notes, which can be grouped into three groups of four, or four groups of three.

The word *meter* is from the Latin *metrum* and Greek *metron,* meaning to measure. A measure in music is a measure of notes, a sum of beats. In 4/4 time, each bar is a sum of four beats. In music, instead of numbers of apples and oranges, we add, subtract, divide, and multiply numbers of beats. Instead of quantities of a liquid or solid, we work with quantities of time. Mathematics is all about relationships of quantities and frequencies. So is music. Musical structure is analyzed by shapes, numbers, and forms. You can get as analytically mathematical and scientific as you want about music, and many theorists have.

Pythagoras, the father of mathematical theory in musical practice, is credited with the notion that the relationship of measurements has musical significance. He discovered that numerical ratios correspond to musical intervals by observing vibrating strings. If we take a string of a certain length, weight, and tension and pluck it, we hear a certain pitch. He discovered that if we divide the string in half, we produce an octave above it, which is the string vibrating exactly twice as fast. If we divide that half in half and pluck the string we produce a pitch two octaves above the whole string, and that short bit of string is vibrating four times faster than the whole string. He went on to determine that if we pinch the string one fourth of the way from one end to the other, and pluck the longer of the two sections of string, we produce a perfect fifth above the whole string.

As discussed in "The Relationship of Pulse and Pitch," page 1▪13 in Book One, the mathematical relationships can all be written out—every harmonic relationship has a mathematical relationship. Division and multiplication make music.

Pythagoras was also interested in the music of the spheres, involving the science of astronomy and physics. Every planetary object is orbiting around the sun at a certain frequency, so it produces a certain interstellar pitch. The tones of the planets have harmonic relationships to all the others, and exist in some musical harmony with each other.

Physics is the study of the properties of matter and energy: wave forms, frequencies, pulses, periods, oscillations—the same phenomena that music is made of. In contemporary quantum physics, we know that subatomic particles exist in a quantum state, which is to say they exist at a certain discrete frequency. When they change energy states, they do not oscillate at a slightly slower or faster rate, but jump to a certain discrete frequency that has a harmonic relationship to the other frequency. One can think of the particles of atoms and molecules being in harmony with themselves. If they are forced out of harmony they explode in the dissonance of atomic fission.

Geometry has to do with shapes, and the geometry of music has to do with the time divided into shapes. Geometry, from *geo* meaning earth and *metrum*, measure, is the measure of shapes. So we can think of the geometry of music as the shapes of music, the measure of phrases, and the forms of music, including sonata, fugue, the dance forms—what have you. We can imagine different kinds of music being associated with different geometries. Some contemporary music can be associated with chaos theory and fractal geometry. Spirals inspired Bartók. He kept a pinecone on his desk and was almost obsessed with the formal structure of his music. In older musical forms you hear a simpler geometry. Music of Bach and Mozart is admired for the perfection of its structure.

While the study of math won't necessarily help you keep a steady pulse, it's somehow reassuring to know that the universe is so musical, and that music is so universal.

The Author

Andrew Lewis has extensive experience in many worlds of music.

In the classical world, he is now in his 17th year as substitute percussionist/timpanist with the San Francisco Symphony, including one season as Principal Timpanist. He has performed as timpanist with the New Zealand Symphony, the Mexico City Symphony, and two years with the National Orchestra of Colombia. You can hear him as timpanist on the San Francisco Symphony's recordings (with Herbert Bloomstedt conducting) of Beethoven's first and third symphonies, Schubert's "Unfinished," and the Grammy Award–winning *Carmina Burana*.

He has performed contemporary chamber music throughout his career and has worked with John Adams, Steve Reich, Elliott Carter, Frank Zappa, Charles Wourinen, Wayne Peterson, Lou Harrison, and Pierre Boulez.

Equally at home in the jazz and rock worlds as a drumset and percussion player, he has played with Ritchie Havens, Ray Charles, and Ella Fitzgerald; worked on Broadway in New York; and been a member of many rock bands, sharing the stage with Moby Grape and the Grateful Dead. He also led the A. C. Lewis Jazz Trio for many years.

As a soloist on both marimba and timpani, he has performed with orchestras, given many recitals, and toured internationally. He also wrote and performed a concerto for percussion and orchestra, which received a warm review from the *New York Times*.

His roots are in ethnic and world music. He began his drumming on conga drums, then tabla. He has traveled extensively, studying African music, South American music in Colombia, Balinese music in Bali, and Indian music in India.

He has been teaching drumset and percussion for 30 years, and more recently has been leading rhythm seminars.

Lewis's formal musical education began at the San Francisco Conservatory of Music, where he earned a bachelor's degree. He earned another bachelor's, and a master's, at the Juilliard School, and went on to earn a postgraduate diploma at Mannes College of Music.

Presently living and freelancing in the San Francisco Bay Area, he is developing a new patented line of metronomes, and runs a rock, jazz, and world music fusion band called Deep Hip Pocket. Please take a look/listen, and contact Mr. Lewis through the website www.rhythmsource.com.

Resources

Apel, Willi, and Daniel, Ralph T. *The Harvard Brief Dictionary of Music.* Cambridge, Mass.: Harvard University Press, 1960.

Friend, Joseph H., and others (eds.). *Webster's New World Dictionary of the American Language.* Cleveland and New York: World Publishing Company, 1960.

Gottleib, Gordon. "Making Friends with the Click Track." *Modern Percussionist,* September 1985, 40–41.

Harris, William H., and Levey, Judith S. (eds.). *The New Columbia Encyclopedia.* (4th ed.) New York: Columbia University Press, 1975.

March, Robert H. *Physics for Poets.* New York: McGraw-Hill, 1983.

McArthur, Tom, and McArthur, Feri (eds.). *Oxford Companion to the Service Language.* New York: Oxford University Press, 1992.

Onions, C. T. (ed.). *Oxford Dictionary of English Etymology.* New York: Oxford University Press, 1966.

Oxford English Dictionary. Oxford: Oxford University Press, 1981.

Sadie, Stanley and Tyrrell, John (eds.). *The New Grove Dictionary of Music and Musicians.* (2nd ed.) New York: Oxford University Press, 2001.

White, Harvey E., and White, Donald H. *Physics and Music: The Science of Musical Sound.* Philadelphia: Saunders College Publications, 1980.

Wood, Alexander. *The Physics of Music.* London: Metheun, 1962.

Zukov, Gary. *The Dancing Wu Li Masters: An Overview of New Physics.* Bantam New Age Books, 1980.

Notes

Notes

Notes

Notes

NOTES

Notes

Notes